MARKETING
MULTIPLIED

A REAL-WORLD GUIDE TO CHANNEL MARKETING FOR
BEGINNERS, PRACTITIONERS, AND EXECUTIVES

MARKETING
MULTIPLIED

Mike Moore | Peter Thomas

Marketing Multiplied

*A Real-World Guide to Channel Marketing
for Beginners, Practitioners, and Executives*

Mike Moore & Peter Thomas

FIRST EDITION

Hardcover ISBN: 978-0-9997748-0-9
Paperback ISBN: 978-0-9997748-1-6
eBook ISBN: 978-0-9997748-2-3

Library of Congress Control Number: 2017964645

Cover art and design by Russell Calhoun

Franklin Kennedy Press

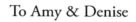

To Amy & Denise

CONTENTS

INTRODUCTION

When we began writing this book, we had a specific audience in mind: the channel marketer. It was to be a book just for those who have found themselves in a channel marketing role within their companies. That's how it happens: You sort of "find" yourself in the role one day. Nobody goes to school for channel marketing and the field isn't covered thoroughly, if at all, by most college marketing programs. The average person on the street doesn't even know what channel marketing is. Contrast that with "teacher" or "civil engineer." Those occupations come with standards in place. We can all agree on what it means to be a teacher or a civil engineer but hardly any of us agree on what it means to be a channel marketer.

That's not surprising when you consider that within the field, there's no clear-cut definition of what channel marketing is. There isn't even a consensus on what to call the category; some call it "local marketing," others call it "partner marketing," "affiliate marketing," "alliance marketing," or other terms. We knew the need was there for a book that offered solid, real-world ideas that could benefit a channel marketer whether she was new to her role or had been in it for some time. The lack of useful information about our field was discouraging and our goal was to rectify that.

But a funny thing happened as we began circulating early drafts to our colleagues. The overall sentiment seemed to be this: yes, this book would be useful to our chosen audience but it could be just as helpful to others whose duties include working with channel marketers—company executives included. Channel marketing suffers from such a low profile and there is so little available practical information that the book might be valuable to people in the organization who *aren't* in channel marketing.

So, if you're an executive reading this—a CMO, perhaps—thank you for taking the time to learn more about an indispensable part of your organization. We're confident that your investment in reading this book will pay dividends and help you better engage your indirect marketing team.

If you're a channel marketer, rest assured we wrote this with you in mind but the takeaway is this: there are others within your company who will benefit from the ideas and best practices we discuss. We don't expect that you'll be able to convince them to read along but we're going to give you the tools you'll need to engage them to create better alignment. We're going to help you find ways to teach them to understand your unique needs.

If you're like many channel marketers, you can probably relate to Janet, a client of ours. Janet oversees channel marketing for her company, which happens to be a multibillion-dollar corporation with thousands of employees and thousands of channel partners. Janet is expected to create programs, run campaigns, and generate thousands of opportunities a year through these partners. The size of her department? Just Janet. Acting as a one-woman marketing agency, wrapped up in the day-to-day details of working with thousands of channel partners, Janet just doesn't have the time or the resources to create what she needs, which are programs that are scalable and repeatable. She needs to be able to develop reusable programs that can support the needs of thousands of channel partners.

Organizations that have a significant amount of channel business don't always staff the channel team or budget appropriately. So, how do you overcome this? In our experience, having a methodology—the way in which you view and organize your world, and a framework that others can buy into and support—can give you the means to be successful no matter how outnumbered and underfunded you are. The key is in logically presenting all of this, which will help you secure a budget for it. We're going to give you the tools you'll need to be able to craft your plan and articulate your channel marketing strategy. Good companies want to invest in good plans, and you'll learn how to develop one you can be proud of.

The overarching fact is this: channel marketing teams are often stuck three to five years behind the rest of the marketing field. Some of this, as we discuss, is because direct marketing is more on the front lines than indirect marketing, so they see the trends first. But some of it is because channel marketers often just don't have the resources and information to keep up. We're going to help you shorten that gap and help you accelerate your efforts. We're going to help you get unstuck.

This book represents a synthesis of best practices that we've learned over the years from both real-world experiences and by hundreds of conversations we've had with channel marketers about the problems they face. You'll learn of the four partner-marketing motions and how to successfully develop them, particularly in the context of the modern buyer's journey. You'll learn how to get your partners to engage, how to measure for success, how to troubleshoot your programs, how to hire and motivate channel marketers, and how to build your channel marketing toolbox.

Whether you're an experienced channel marketer looking to hone your craft, someone new to the field looking to deepen your understanding of it, or a seasoned marketing executive who knows there's untapped potential in your company's channel, we're grateful to have the opportunity to explore this challenging field with you.

We have three goals for this book:

1. We want to provide you with a framework to efficiently organize your marketing efforts.

2. We want to give you practical tools and resources you can apply to your business today and refer to when stuck.

3. We want to extend the book experience into an online community that will help you with ideas and inspiration as the market changes.

Toward our final goal, you'll find all the resources, frameworks, and examples at *www.marketingmultiplied-book.com*. Thanks for reading and welcome to the start of what we know will be an extraordinary journey.

—Mike and Peter

CHAPTER ONE

WHAT IS CHANNEL MARKETING?

In his groundbreaking book *Let's Get Real or Let's Not Play: Transforming the Buyer/Seller Relationship*, Mahan Khalsa wrote: "We often mistake fluency (in which we both use the words easily) with comprehension (when we both have the same meanings for the words)." The words "channel marketing" mean different things to different people, so we want to share our definition early. Channel marketing is a specialization within the overall discipline of marketing focused on communicating value *to, with, through*, and *for* channel partners.

Channel marketing: a specialization within the overall discipline of marketing focused on communicating value *to, with, through,* and *for* channel partners.

And who are channel partners? *Channel partners* are companies outside of your organization that sell, service, or refer your products, often bundling value-added services. They might be distributors, resellers, agents, alliance partners, independent hardware/software/cloud vendors, service providers, or any one of a multitude of third-party companies. And though we use the term "channel marketing" throughout this book, it's important to understand that the principles are essentially the same across any indirect distribution model, including franchises and affinity businesses. And while many of our examples are from our experience in the technology industry, these concepts apply to all vertical industries. No matter the form of "partner," you, as a channel marketer, are in a unique position to help them, and our goal is to teach you how.

The Power of Scale

What's the value of a strong partner network? A few years back, Mike was fortunate to work for Microsoft as part of an events team. They were executing several hundred events per year, and the events were successful in terms of attendance and driving sales pipeline. So successful, in fact, that the VP of Mike's business unit wondered aloud in a meeting one day how the company could unlock the potential of having the thousands of Microsoft partners do similar Microsoft-themed events, too. This inspired Mike to create a program that helped, supported, and encouraged Microsoft's channel partners to hold technical summits, seminars, webinars, and workshops. Within one year of the launch, Microsoft partners collectively delivered more than *5,000* events. Partners who participated in the program showed faster sales growth than partners who did not, and they reported higher satisfaction with their Microsoft partnership.

Mike was able to use the resources of Microsoft to produce a sustainable marketing program that was scalable across the entire partnership network. This is the difference between being mired in one-off solutions, and leveraging a repeatable solution for use by all your channel partners. That difference can make a substantial impact on your company, and a bigger impact on your quality of life.

Lack of Recognition

But not every company is Microsoft. One challenge (which you might already have noticed if you've spent any time in this field) is a certain degree of unfamiliarity on the part of the marketing departments of many organizations when it comes to the channel. Some companies go to market almost exclusively through the channel and, in those cases, the channel receives more visibility. Others employ a hybrid direct/indirect route to market. For those, the lack of recognition of the importance of channel enablement can equate to a lack of perceived value by executives and sales teams.

The Effectiveness of Your Channel Partners

Even in organizations that recognize the importance of channel marketing, we still find there's disagreement on the ideal partner profile, what to measure, the content mix or "right" amount of content, or even what doing "a good job" means. There's no guide for how much or how little market development funds (MDF) to give to partners, or how to measure the effectiveness of an MDF program.[1] While there is broad agreement that sales incentives can be motivational for partners, the optimal mix of these incentives remains debatable. And so, there's a kind of paralysis that results in missed opportunities and doing just enough to get by. But proactive companies forge ahead regardless, creating programs to reach and activate channel partners in highly scalable ways. These are the companies that benefit from the sales and marketing capacity of those channel partners.

At its core, the success of a channel program depends on the effectiveness of your partners. Your job is to help *them* succeed with *your* product or service. Just because someone agrees to be your partner, it doesn't mean they're going to bring your product to market proactively. When it comes to your channel

---

[1]   We'll examine the topic of MDF in Chapter 8.

partners, you should ask and answer two critical questions: what's in it for them, and why should they care? In other words, of all the vendors whose products your partners could sell[2] (including your competitors), why should your partners pick *you?* Remember the very first part of our definition: channel marketing is about communicating value *to* your partners. The *with*, *through*, and *for* will follow.

The Four Partner-Marketing Motions and the Modern Buyer

As this book unfolds, we'll talk about *to*, *with*, *through*, and *for* within the context of the four actions that are required to obtain happy customers: attract, convert, close, and delight.[3] We'll share a channel marketing methodology that maps to the modern buyer's journey. And we're going to put a heavy emphasis on *learning* content, the most critical and overlooked element of many integrated campaigns.

Regarding the "modern" buyer: What you'll read in the following chapters represents our response to the idea that, in addition to the lack of definition, channel marketing as a discipline is woefully behind the times. Many of the tactics in use are outdated and they don't properly align with how people buy today. Much has been said and written about the digital disruption and how buying behavior has changed over

---

[2]   We'll use the term "sell" loosely throughout this book. By this, we mean any value-added activity a partner combines with your product or service.

[3]   As first outlined by Brian Halligan and Dharmesh Shah of Hubspot in their seminal work, *Inbound Marketing: Attract, Engage, and Delight Customers Online* (Wiley, 2009). We'll use slightly different nomenclature, as you'll see.

the past twenty years. We're in a buyer's economy, yet many companies still don't understand this and are being left behind. If your channel partners are relying on the same tired outbound marketing tactics such as mass emailing and telemarketing, they're missing out.

There's a disconnect between the way most businesses look to sell their products or services and the way today's prospects want to buy. Channel marketers must be cognizant of this disconnect and help their partners overcome it. As a channel marketer, you know the pressure you're under to enable your partners to produce leads (qualified leads, no less) from executives, sales teams, field marketing, and partners. They may ask in different ways but for your internal stakeholders and channel partners, it almost always boils down to the same request: *Give me more leads.*

Here's how it usually sounds:

- **Executive:** "How many leads did we generate this [month, quarter, year]?"
- **Field Marketing:** "I need content that works in my region, so my partners can generate leads."
- **Field Sales:** "The leads you're giving me are useless. Give me better leads for a change."
- **Partners:** "Give me leads that are ready to buy."

For the prospects at the receiving end of your marketing, however, the story is different. They just want you (and your partners) to chill out. They'll find you when they're ready!

When was the last time you answered a cold call? And if you did, were you happy to talk to the salesperson on the other end of the line? How much spam do you get each day? When was the last time you opened one of those emails, let alone clicked the call to action? How about those blow-in flyers from your bank that come with your monthly statement? Do you even catch a glimpse of the offer as you're recycling the flyer?

That's how your prospects feel. They don't care about phone calls, emails, or direct mail because they're just not ready. Consider your behavior as a consumer. When you sit down to make your next big purchase or plan your next vacation, where are you going to start? Google, of course, or in the case of a vacation, TripAdvisor. That's where we all start. Fifteen years ago, this was not true. Back then the salesperson was in control of the sale. They were the gatekeeper of the information, and if you wanted to know something, you had to talk with them.

Modern buyers exhibit three fundamental behaviors: learning, shopping, and buying. Successful marketing today aligns the seller's actions to the buyer's behavior. Carried out correctly, the buyer learns from the seller over time, develops a level of trust in the seller's subject matter authority, and ultimately trusts the seller with their dollars. **Learn, shop, buy**. Once a customer, they share their satisfaction with others and **recommend** the product/solution to friends and colleagues, which is the fourth (and arguably most important) behavior of buyers.

With sixty-eight percent of buyers saying they prefer to research products online and sixty percent saying they don't want to interact with a salesperson at all,[4] it's critically important

---

[4] "The B2B eCommerce Playbook For 2017," Forrester Research, 2017.

to allow prospective buyers access to your information on their terms. Most importantly, that means no sales pitch! Succesful alignment results in a teaching moment (think of those 5,000 Microsoft events), which breeds both credibility and loyalty. *In the modern economy, those that teach earn the right to sell.* When it's time to buy, it's you the prospect remembers.

Easier Said than Done

You probably know all of this, at least on some level, and we know what you're facing. Most marketers carry a quota, typically marketing qualified leads, or MQLs. There is pressure to deliver on those numbers quarter after quarter and there's also a finite amount of budget for campaigns and activities. Year over year, the quota increases and the budget decreases. Even if the marketer knows that the right thing to do is to execute a teaching campaign that drives awareness and never pitches a product, there's a risk. The prospect may learn something from them and buy from someone else, in which case the marketer risks not hitting the quota. What if the campaign successfully teaches but generates no leads?

Wanting to mitigate the risk, the marketer then doubles down on shopping and buying content, pitching away.[5] But you can't just show up on someone's door and propose marriage; it takes time to build trust. So, the numbers are bleak, but they're enough to make the quota, so no one loses their job.

The numbers are weak because most of the prospects the marketer wants to reach won't trust them since the prospects

---

have received nothing of value that would establish trust. Today's buyers are savvier (even more cynical) than ever before. They can smell a sales pitch from a mile away, and it's a big turn-off.

If this sounds like your company and your channel, we understand. You're not alone. We're going to give you a framework that helps you align your partners around the modern buyer's journey. Change won't happen overnight because you won't be able to get everyone on board at once. But that's okay; there will be short-term goals and long-term goals and only you know how much and how fast you can push to make things happen within your organization. In the short term, we'll recommend you keep doing what you've been doing because that generates the leads that feed the machine and, eventually, your long plays will catch up and you'll have enough leads to supply the entire organization and your partners.

We hope you find the possibilities exciting. There's a lot of work to do but we're going to break it all down—for you, your organization, and your channel. We're going to explore the nuances of the channel and help you find ways to unleash its potential.

CHAPTER TWO

TO, WITH, THROUGH, AND FOR PARTNER MARKETING

Recently, we had a conversation with the VP of channels for a small software company who had several strategic initiatives, and all of them were Priority #1. He wanted to increase the number of partners in the program; introduce a new partner portal, a training and certification program, and a through-partner demand generation platform, all at the same time. His team consisted of himself and a part-time consultant. He had no lack of ambition, but what surprised us most was his attitude. When we talked to him about his channel, he stated that the partners he had were "lucky to have the opportunity to sell our products. If they can't see the value in our program, I don't see how that's our problem; we'll simply find partners that do." We were surprised by how self-centered, and not partner-centered, his company was. We find other examples of this at channel conferences where we sometimes hear speakers and attendees talking at length about "thinning the herd." Kicking partners out of their programs, in other words.

Channel leaders frequently forget that a channel partnership is a *relationship*. And like any relationship, it needs to be nurtured and cared for. You *cannot* take it for granted. In the example above with the VP of channels, he mentioned that his company had no less than fifteen direct competitors. So sure was he that his products were superior (and for all we know they might be) that he downplayed the risk that his channel partners would ever lead with a competitor's product. But the fact is, his channel partners weren't moving his products as efficiently as they could have been. Eliminating channel partners certainly wasn't going to help and adding more partners might have helped but only marginally. Though he refused to see it, nothing was going to improve for this channel VP if his company's one-sided approach remained.

We understand that there will always be some segment of the partner population that is unproductive, and, to some extent, a drain on the program. Partners require resources to manage, even if you're as low-touch as possible. This problem serves as the inspiration for the "thinning the herd" conversation.

But the common denominator in both cases is this: the partners are taken for granted.

Relationship Dynamics

Successful partnering comes down to the same fundamentals that govern every relationship. You don't get married and then stop giving your spouse a birthday gift. You don't start a friendship by saying, "What can you do for me?" You nurture your marriage. You go into a friendship with no agenda other than, if you're fortunate, getting the other person to call you a friend in return. You treat people you are involved with as equals. Even an employer/employee relationship works best with mutual respect and a shared idea of what you both, together, can accomplish.

Successful partnerships happen when each partner recognizes the value that the other brings to the table. If you provide something—creating teaching moments, for instance, that educate your partners and help them succeed—then you earn the right to do business with them. Providing value is the foundation of successful partnering.

Successful partnerships happen when each partner recognizes the value that the other brings to the table.

So, how can you help your partners? How can you bring out the best in them? These are the questions that, when answered, lead to successful partnerships with favorable results. Let's consider the four ways in which brands go to market with their channels:

- *To* their partners
- *With* their partners
- *Through* their partners
- *For* their partners

To-Partner Marketing

To-partner channel marketing is mainly about providing the partner with a reason to work with you. It's based, like so much of sales and marketing, on empathy. It's conveying to the partner what's in it *for them*. It's giving them a reason to care and to think about your brand.

Successful to-partner marketing is treating your partners like customers.

To-partner marketing is often overlooked. There's an assumption that once a partner signs the contract, they will be a partner for life—but this isn't true. Like any consumer, partners have choices.

The Problem with Success

Occasionally, we encounter a company that seems to forget how they got to where they are. They've made it. They're wealthy and powerful, with thousands of employees across the world. Their products are sublime and they have a transformative impact on their customers. Their conferences are well-attended and an A-list speaker always gives the keynote address. They have *arrived*.

If you work for one of these brands, you might find yourself looking at smaller companies, specifically your channel partners, as less successful. You might think they have less to offer and don't sell and execute as well as your business. But this is a dangerous trap. Thinking this way breeds a condescending attitude that poisons the channel, over time changing the way partners see you. A relationship that starts out optimistically can suddenly turn sour, even antagonistic, if either party is self-centered.

Partners are running their own businesses and their problems are different from a brand's problems. Their brand relationships are not the first things on their minds. A channel marketer's job is to **capture and maintain the attention of his or her partners**.

A Partner is a Customer, Too

Another reason to-partner marketing gets overlooked is that brands tend to consider their products only from the end-user perspective. They can easily answer questions about how their product will make someone's life better by her use of it. They love talking in those terms (techs & specs! speeds & feeds!). But they're not nearly as effusive (or convincing) when they're asked to explain how representing the product is worthwhile for a channel partner. From a marketing viewpoint, they spend their time thinking about features and benefits for the end buyer, not the people in between. What's in it for the partner?

Moreover, the channel partner is closer to, and therefore generally more familiar with, the end customer. They know—directly from the source—the customers' needs and the concerns. Your idea of what's relevant to the customer may not align with your partner's view. You may even be entirely accurate in what you think is important but that will mean little to the partner. If a value proposition you're pushing isn't the value proposition that the partner wants to promote, the partner won't sell it. When you're defining your product's features and benefits, you must consider your channel partners as the audience as much (or more) as the end customers.

If you're at all skeptical about this idea, consider the recent examples of companies that have miscalculated the consequences of moving customers to the cloud without adequately explaining what's in it for the channel partners. Data solutions that required on-premise configuration, servicing and support left channel partners behind with cloud versions, not because there wasn't any value remaining for the partners but because the partners were never brought up to speed on how they could participate in that value and continue to get economic benefits. Companies even decommissioned on-site or data center solutions to ramp up their cloud business only to discover their cloud business didn't grow to expectations, leaving both them and their partners in the lurch. Bad things can happen when the concerns of channel partners are overlooked.

It's All About Them

Channel partners are motivated by *their* economic interests, not yours. Marketing *to* them means giving them reasons to listen and act. It also means spelling out to them how their services add value to the equation. What's the biggest financial problem your partner typically has? Not enough business! So, there's your starting point. How can you drive more business to your partners? Try this: Every time you launch a new product or service, involve your partners by conveying to them how the new product or service is going to increase their business.

A product launch, by the way, is a useful way to reactivate stagnant partners. Pull a list of the partners you haven't heard from in a while. Present your next campaign to them in a way that makes it clear not just how great your product is but how wonderful your product launch will be *for them*. Then watch them go from stagnant to energized.[6]

Understanding your partners' motivations means giving them the tools they need to be successful with your products. Brands often refer to this as *partner enablement* (or "partner training" or "partner readiness content"). No matter what you call it, your partners will invest in you if you invest in them. It's simple reciprocity and it's the natural order of the universe. When we receive, we tend to want to give back.

Optimizing your Channel through Segmentation

Of course, not all partners are motivated by the same things in the same way. Sometimes, particularly with big channels, a single approach won't work. Tools that are effective for one type of partner may be less useful, or even irrelevant, for another. You can't be all things to all people. Successful brands get around this by segmenting their efforts, essentially profiling their channels and marketing to them accordingly, much like your direct team does for their to-customer marketing. Group

---

[6]   For a more thorough discussion on how to involve your partners in product launches, see Chapter 4.

A will be reached in one way with one message while Group B gets contacted in another way with a different message.

What we most often see brands do is segment their channel based on sales performance—the typical Gold, Silver, Bronze tiering. While we agree that sales performance is a vital component in segmentation, it's not forward-looking. A better approach is to segment according to the 3 P's: Profiling, Performance, and Potential.

Profiling can be done geographically (by continent, country, region, etc.), by type of partner (reseller versus integrator, for example), by the partner's solution or industry specialization, size (headcount), or by whatever makes sense for your channel. The key is to think of them in the way they think of themselves.

Performance analysis is a review of the number of deals closed, the dollar value of deals, and marketing performance of the partner. It's a look at their historical contribution to the business in a sales and marketing capacity.

Potential is an analysis of their focus, growth plans, resources, and how much a part of their business you are. This metric is particularly useful for partners that are new to your channel and have existing sales and marketing capacity that has yet to be directed to your business.

Once you've completed the segmentation exercise, you now know how to speak to each partner audience. There may be some overlap in the messaging but the calls to action can be different depending on who you're addressing.

Revenue is just one piece of the puzzle

In your to-partner marketing efforts, it is critical that you track your results, and the best measurement for this is in the form of *reach* (i.e., number of partners trained on a program or initiative).[7] Revenue metrics are essential as well but not as important at this stage, as your primary concern in to-partner marketing is in building awareness and getting partners to support your ideas.

Not making revenue the focus can be a challenging mind shift. It's natural to think about the bottom line and to consider only the immediate results. Spending money on a to-partner campaign almost certainly won't provide the quick return you'd prefer but it is a worthwhile investment. We know it's easier to imagine that your partners are all engaged, that you can just roll out your new product, service, or campaign, and your partners will take it from there. But this "if you build it they will come" approach will prove costly in the long run.

Remember: your channel partners aren't sitting around just looking for ways to help you. They've got their own problems, their own interests, and their own sets of motivations. Understanding what drives them is the first step toward successful to-partner marketing.

Go through a partner persona-building exercise with your team.

- What are the roles within the partner's organization that you need to speak with? For example, Executive, Sales & Marketing, and Technical.

- Build a to-partner communication plan, which includes a marketing calendar, programs, messages, and tactics.

---

[7] For more information on "reach" (as well as "frequency" and "yield") see Chapter 10.

With-Partner Marketing

With-partner marketing has you and your channel partner shoulder to shoulder, going to market together. For example, a seminar where both companies are presenters, both logos are displayed side-by-side, and both companies drive attendance. Together, you're selling to the end-user. Or a product launch where you provide the event and multiple partners simultaneously drive demand for it.

The Better-Together Story

Sometimes two organizations with complementary products can go to market together, providing a joint solution. Your product and your partner's service offering, for instance. Sure, the end-user can purchase the two pieces separately but they may never think to do so. Presenting the pieces as parts of a single solution could prove advantageous to both brand and partner. A good example to consider is a cloud storage solution. A customer moving from on-premise storage to the cloud finds a storage solution much more valuable with a channel partner there to help migrate the data, create permission schemes for user access, provide training, install to users' desktops, and do whatever else is necessary to ensure a smooth transition for the customer.

Joint marketing initiatives where you're lending a channel partner the power of your brand can be very rewarding for a channel. Most channel partners are smaller than you, and having the recognition of your name gives them credibility and creates a "halo" effect. This is why channel partners appreciate with-partner marketing more than brands do. Brands perceive fewer benefits for themselves (they must build the content, promote it, get partners to participate, etc.). But of course, this gets back to the premise at the start of this chapter—bringing out the best in your partners and earning their continued loyalty. It's the first half of the reciprocity equation: make your partners look good and they'll return the favor.

Picking Winners

A legitimate concern here, however, is how to scale this approach. If you've got hundreds of partners or more, it may not be practical to assume you can engage in joint marketing initiatives with all of them. So, how do you choose? Sometimes it's a matter of orienting around customer needs—where can you best serve the customers by taking your message to them jointly? Where can you attract the most interest? Some opportunities are better than others and you probably already know what those are. Some organizations choose by responding to their partners' requests, using an application process where a partner can essentially make a pitch that your help will be worth the time and resources. Some organizations use surveys to determine how much of a marketing budget their partners work with and how much of each partner's resources are dedicated to the brand's solution. This allows you to see which partners are more capable and, therefore, better candidates for your time and money. Often, the commitment level by the partner helps make the decision. You might decide that if a partner is willing to do what it takes to get a room full of prospects together, then you're willing to be there on behalf of the brand. You can set KPIs to quantitatively measure your partners' levels of commitment and respond with your participation appropriately.

> **Practice:** Build a joint value proposition with your partners. How are you better together? How can you make 1 + 1 = 3? Consider, for example, the Microsoft/HP joint story: Microsoft software running on HP hardware. Combining these solutions solves a customer need, as opposed to forcing the customer to consider both Microsoft and HP separately.

Through-Partner Marketing

Through-partner marketing is where you give your partners the content and training for them to deliver your message to the market all on their own.

Freedom to Succeed

Letting your partners take your content and run with it, and making it easy for them to do so, allows you to enjoy the multiplying effect of the channel. You need to create interactive campaigns that they can modify to suit their voice and customer profile, and create content that allows room for the partner's logo and value proposition. Instead of creating content built around your brand, think about creating content built around your partner and *their* brands, allowing each of them to tell their unique story.

Through-partner marketing is giving your partners the ability to succeed with your content in their way and in their world. It requires latitude, which, unfortunately, isn't always appreciated by those responsible for managing the brand. Naturally, they're protective, and there's a perceived risk that partners will misuse or misrepresent the brand. Sometimes, the first challenge is helping people in your organization to see that enabling your channel partners with co-branded content is a risk worth taking. Might there be dilution (or even some downright mutation) of the brand? Maybe. But what's the tradeoff?

If you don't allow your partners to make use of your content in a way that works for them, you risk two things. First, they might just decide to go to market with another brand's content, one that's a little more flexible and a little less protective. Second, they might just use your content anyway and with less than quality results. When you see an old, low-resolution version of your logo on material that isn't even accurate, you're going to wish you'd given permission in the first place and worked a little closer with your partner to make sure they're using your material in a way that best represents your brand. Permission, along with some decent guidelines and a little training, can help you better maintain the brand than trying to keep your partner from using it at all.

Think of it this way. Mike's eleven-year-old son likes to offer to help mow the lawn. Sure, the cutting paths aren't always straight, and sometimes there's a patch or two that gets missed. Nevertheless, Mike is grateful for the initiative, and he understands the long-term benefits of getting his son involved in the house chores. The tradeoff is worth it. Your organization needs to see its partners in the same light.

Getting Started: Enable your partners to share information online and launch your message with their unique spin into the market. A good first step would be to give your partners content they can easily share on their website. Consider what the message needs to be, how it's presented, any calls to action or offers, and how best to package it up and deliver it to your partners.

For-Partner Marketing

For-partner marketing is just how it sounds: You market *for* your partner. Most organizations engage in some level of for-partner marketing but many do it ineffectively. They wait to hear from their partners and respond when their partners ask for something, like content or collateral material. It's a reactive approach. Far more useful is *proactive* for-partner marketing.

Why Make Them Ask?

Proactive for-partner marketing includes creating campaigns to drive demand and generating leads for your partners, saving them the effort and expense of doing the execution themselves. It could mean assigning a channel account manager (CAM) to work with a specific group of partners, all connected by industry or geography, for instance. Ideally, the CAM should be supported by a partner marketing manager (PMM), allowing the CAM to launch demand generation campaigns for partners or host a local event on their behalf. The CAM's targets should be based not on sales or revenue, but on leads generated, events hosted, or partners contacted.

As you no doubt suspect, for-partner marketing is very popular with partners! Their responsibility becomes focused on closing deals, not generating leads. It's an approach that makes a lot of sense when you think about it. After all, you have the brand awareness, the expertise in communicating the value of your message to the market, and the ability and infrastructure in place to collect leads. Your partners don't have these capabilities, at least not to the degree in which you have them, and this is especially true with new or recently-acquired partners. Naturally, such partners will require more hand-holding.

It's the right approach (sometimes the only one) for referral partners, too. These are the partners who just refer your product or service opportunistically. Your solution is tangential to their core business, but opportunities arise from time to time. Think of a CPA, for example, who might come across the opportunity to refer a brand of tax preparation software to a client. He's probably not going to make selling tax preparation software a high priority but, if he sees an opportunity, he'll likely refer the software and happily collect a commission. With these types of partners, you're going to have to do the heavy lifting for them.

For-partner marketing does have its drawbacks. It's much more labor-intensive, obviously. It also comes with the risk of breeding a level of entitlement. "Where are my leads?!" can become a familiar refrain as partners look exclusively to you, abandoning their own efforts to generate interest in your brand. And so, we return to relationship dynamics once again. In the end, you'll have to decide if marketing *for* your partners makes sense for your organization's goals.

Whatever your approach to your channel—to, with, through, or for your partners—the key is helping your partners so that they can help you. Yes, they're lucky to have access to your products. But you're fortunate to have them, too, and your job is to bring out the best in them. Start with zero expectations, work hard to earn their attention, provide them with the training and tools to help them win, and watch both of your businesses grow.

CHAPTER THREE

THE MODERN BUYER'S JOURNEY

How brands market with their partners (i.e., to, with, through, and for) are avenues that ultimately lead to interaction with the end-customer in the form of purchase. But to understand *that* interaction, one needs to understand the factors that influence every sale.

We talked in Chapter 1 about how the digital world has altered buying behavior. Most buying decisions today start with a Google search, and there's seemingly no limit to the amount of information available to a buyer—information that used to exist only in the mind of a salesperson. Before the internet, if you wanted to learn about a new car you were thinking of buying, you had to go to your local dealership. If you wanted to make vacation plans, you had to call a travel agent. The seller controlled the buying script, and marketers used traditional outbound marketing tactics such as direct mail, cold calling, and advertising to drive people to the store.

Buying is radically different now, and so much has been written about it that it's practically common knowledge. For readers wanting to explore this transition in depth, we recommend Seth Godin's excellent book *Permission Marketing: Turning Strangers Into Friends And Friends Into Customers*.

Inbound Marketing

Inbound marketing is a response to the reality of today's marketplace, a methodology oriented around how modern buyers learn and then make their purchasing decisions. Inbound marketing is grounded in tactics that earn customer attention by offering useful content that attracts customers and keeps them coming back for more. In their seminal book *Inbound Marketing:*

Attract, Engage, and Delight Customers Online, Brian Halligan and Dharmesh Shah describe the four actions successful companies use to obtain visitors, leads, customers, and promoters. These steps are *attract, convert, close, delight,* and they represent the dominant thinking of the modern transactional process.

And yet, these actions—attract, convert, close, delight—don't reflect the modern buyer's journey so much as define a *seller's proper response* to the modern buyer's journey. Looking at this process strictly from a buyer's perspective yields a different point of view. We're going to approach the behavior of today's buyers by considering *their* specific actions: *learning, shopping, buying,* and *recommending.* These are the modern buyer's actions, which, in turn, lead to the respective seller's actions Halligan and Shah describe.

Why People Buy

Let's pause for a moment to acknowledge the fact that there are two reasons why people buy any product or service:[8]

1. The need to avoid pain (or loss)

2. The need to gain pleasure

Consumers make purchases to satisfy one of these two primary requirements and, in some cases, both. In the most cynical terms, the job of every seller is to amplify the pain (fear of missing out, loss of money, time, or standing) and the gain (increased revenue, favor, and promotion), with the goal of driving the prospect to take a specific action.

---

[8] Klein, Jim, "Discover the 2 Reasons Why People Buy Any Product or Service," Web, National Association of Sales Professionals, *https://www.nasp.com/.*

With this in mind, let's return to the buyer's behavior along the continuum.

Learning

Learning is where every purchase begins. We are always in learning mode. We do it every day, whether we're consciously looking to buy something or not. We read articles, blogs, trade journals, and industry websites. We converse with others with similar interests on social networks. We follow trends and discover new products. Every day, we're learning something new.

Then one day, recalling the buyer motivations above, we happen upon a solution to a problem we have, or a way to enhance our position. Before this discovery, we might have had no idea that such a solution (or improvement) existed. We might not have even known we had a problem in the first lace.

This represents the start of today's buying process. The inspiration to purchase can come from many places, and the buyer's journey is anything but linear. Buyers meander through the internet and interact with peers, friends, and family, and absorb the information that is presented to them, here and there taking small actions that might eventually lead to a purchase. It is for this reason ad retargeting has proven to be an effective tactic; people spend a lot of time on their social networks and other places on the web, and seeing the same message repeatedly (especially one that teaches through short-form video) gives the prospect a sense of familiarity with the brand.

Prospects are always learning, so it's imperative that brands and channel partners are positioned to share information. They must be ready to teach.

Shopping

When we're shopping, we're already aware that there's a solution to our pain or an opportunity for gain. We've become enlightened to a possibility we didn't know existed before, and now it's on the front burner.

We might even wonder how we've gotten along this far without it! We see this all the time with software. A software solution is typically a response to an unspoken (or unconscious) question: *Isn't there a better, more efficient, way?* When we discover that it exists, even if we weren't consciously looking for it, we've got to have it. We reach a point where the light bulb goes on and we go from "learning" to "shopping."

For many buyers, this moment leads to the consideration of alternative solutions. There are always options: should I choose Solution A or Solution B?

Buying

Buying is the moment of truth. Sales professionals often forget that, especially for large enterprise deals, buyers grapple with a significant amount of fear, uncertainty, and doubt at the point at which the proverbial trigger is about to be pulled. Sellers are around their products and services all day, every day. They're so familiar with them that no matter what the asking prices are, they seem like reasonable amounts. For a buyer of that product or service, however, it might be their very first experience buying it or spending that amount of money. Indeed, as we've discussed, they may have only recently learned of its existence!

Careers are made or broken with this buying decision. It's a Big Moment, and the seller must recognize its significance.

The buying process, therefore, must include *validation* and *confirmation*. A buyer needs to be assured he or she is making the right choice.

The Committee

Additionally, the complexity of the sales cycle has increased in recent years. The buying decision, fraught as it is with uncertainty, is often shared among multiple participants as opposed to a single decision-maker. In their groundbreaking book *The Challenger Sale*, Matthew Dixon and Brent Adamson explore this phenomenon in detail. They call it "The Rise of the Consensus-Based Sale," and they describe how "C-level executives with significant decision-making authority are unwilling to go out on a limb to make a large purchase decision without the support of their teams."[9] From a seller's standpoint, this means not only dealing with many potential influencers but dealing with influencers who may be at dissimilar stages of the buying process. One might be ready to buy while another is still shopping and yet another is still learning.

Recommending

Congratulations, you've earned a customer! She has learned, shopped, and bought, and if all has gone well, she's feeling a certain amount of pride in having completed this journey, and in having made the tough, but correct, decision.

This is the green field of opportunities, as this buyer represents a prime source of referral business. Unfortunately, this

---

[9]   Adamson, Brent; Dixon, Matthew, *The Challenger Sale: Taking Control of the Customer Conversation*, Portfolio, 2011.

is also the point at which many sellers drop the ball. Sales compensation plans often incentivize the rep to focus on new customer acquisition, or hunting, rather than farming for new deals among existing customers. Old accounts—even the one that came in just yesterday morning—are de-emphasized in favor of the promise of fresh territory.

Let's return to the *learning* portion of the journey. The social networking and the interaction with peers, friends, and family is an integral part of it. When we're happy with a purchase we've made, we talk about it on Facebook, on LinkedIn, over lunch, and over drinks. Potential buyers learn from word-of-mouth.

This feedback from others becomes even more critical in the "shopping" phase. The choice between Solution A and Solution B? It's often validated by the recommendation of a trusted friend or advisor, or even a group of strangers, so long as they are unified in their opinion and qualified to give it (think TripAdvisor and Yelp!). According to one recent study, recommendations are the primary influencing factor across all stages of the purchase cycle, from initial awareness of a product right on through to the actual purchase decision.[10] A solid recommendation is one way to mitigate those feelings of uncertainty and doubt that dog every buyer at the moment of truth.

As evidenced by the rise in influencer marketing campaigns (and the agencies that execute them on a brand's behalf), it's clear that more and more brands are embracing the impact referrals have on their businesses.

---

[10] Keller, Ed, "Recommendations are What Drives Your Business. Remember to Ask for Them," *Fortune*, Web, 25 Jul. 2012.

Okay, so now we're in the buyer's head, looking at the world through the mindset of a potential customer. Let's overlay this with how we interact with our channel partners. How does the modern buyer's journey influence the way we market to our partners, with our partners, through our partners, and for our partners?

CHAPTER FOUR

TO-PARTNER MARKETING

In this chapter, we'll discuss to-partner marketing in the context of the modern buyer's journey. Your partners are a segment of your customers. How will you guide them through the process of *learning, shopping, buying,* and *recommending*?

It's important to realize, by the way, that when we speak of partners, we're not referring merely to your partners' leadership levels. Your to-partner marketing must encompass all the roles and disciplines that deal with your product, from middle management to the sales/marketing/services people. Think of the people on the front lines. *Especially* the people on the front lines. How will your partnership help them in their day-to-day efforts? How can you help the salesperson close more sales? Meet a quota? Make more money, faster? There's more to your partners than just the executive staff. We stress this because we see a lot of partner programs that seem to speak only to the CEO, with the assumption that the CEO will somehow pass the message along. That's an unreliable strategy.

To-Partner: Learning

Keep in mind that the typical buyer's path starts before the specifics of the product or service are discovered, and so it is with your partners. They might be acquainted with your products and services but that doesn't mean they know how your products and services fit within the context of the market or industry. This is obvious in the partner recruiting stage; you must sell your potential partner on the need in the marketplace for what you provide. But it's no less valid with your existing partners and products. Indeed, the assumption that your partners understand the market for your products and services is often wrong.

Besides, the market is always changing, which necessitates a steady flow of messaging to your partner community.

To-partner learning content takes two forms, which we'll classify broadly as *research* and *skill building*.

With **research**, you're providing your partners with industry information, trends, analysis, and ideas. You're keeping them informed and up-to-date on developments that can help them discover opportunities where your products and services can be helpful. It might be published reports from SiriusDecisions, Gartner, Forrester Research, The 2112 Group, or other analyst firms. Many small and medium-sized companies don't have the time or financial resources to subscribe to these kinds of services or do any real research themselves. They depend on you to keep them abreast of what's happening and how it's going to impact their world.

But what you send them needs to be put in context. Nobody wants to be overwhelmed with copious amounts of research, white papers, and eBooks. What's the *message* in the information? What's the key takeaway? What's in it for the partner and what does it mean for their customers? Context is what makes the information both useful and usable to a partner.

Skill building refers to sales and marketing best practice training, where you share ideas that help your partners not just with your product or service, but with their businesses. It's about helping them succeed. They don't have to accept your help, and large partners may have no need. Smaller partners might be perfectly content (and highly successful) operating their companies just as they are. But being able to provide access to operational tips and tools that foster best practices can go a long way in generating loyalty with your partner community.

Brands often neglect this part of the learning stage because they just don't think about it. Others purposely avoid it, believing that if you train a partner to be a better seller, that same partner might sell a competitive product instead. But we say *so what?* If it helps the partner sell the brand's products while strengthening the partner as an organization—everybody wins. The more successful brands see the big picture, understanding that in the long term, helping a partner succeed, in whatever form that takes, ultimately helps the brand as well.

Your partners, like all customers, are in a continual state of learning. They're being bombarded every day with information, some relevant, some not so much. One thing is sure: If they're not learning from you, they're learning from someone else.

To-Partner: Shopping

Through the *learning* phase—hopefully, with your help—your partners come to understand the marketplace and where you fit. They know the problems that their potential customers have, the needs that are unfulfilled, and the opportunities that exist. Your partners are now in *shopping* mode. It's time to make sure your solution is top-of-mind.

Much of this comes down to simple communication—keeping your partners informed about your product developments and keeping them in the loop. You're letting them know you're there when they need you.

This isn't always as easy as it seems. Often there's a disconnect between a brand and its partners, which is an extension of the disconnect between product marketing and channel marketing teams. With new products, the function of product marketing is critical. They are responsible for research, testing, and feedback. What product marketing learns during this process often gets disseminated through direct marketing efforts before the channel marketing team even has a chance to approach partners with it. If a partner learns about the product at the same time as the public, they often feel left out. We can't stress enough how important it is to involve your partners early on in product rollouts. You want your product to be top-of-mind? Let your partners bring it to market *with* you, not *in addition* to you.

Apple is an example of a company that does this well. Every time a new iPhone is set to come out, Apple arms their channel (AT&T, Verizon, Sprint, and others) with a coordinated through-partner campaign that closely aligns with the direct marketing campaign. All end customers see a consistent message and this is especially important because the point of purchase for most consumers is through the channel partner.

Brands that involve their partners reap an added benefit: they get valuable feedback from their partners as they begin to go to market. Partners have a lot of experience and expertise—use this to your advantage. Test-market your solution. Learn the potential objections and tweak your approach accordingly.

Involve your partners in product launches. Give them pre-launch access to the product; let them be the ones to share it with existing customers and prospects. Build your marketing program with this involvement in mind.

To-Partner: Buying

The partner has learned about the needs of the marketplace and knows your solution and how it fits. But they're not going to evangelize it unless, and until, they believe in it. You need your partner's buy-in.

This should be easy, right? They're your partners, after all. They're already on board. Give 'em a product and they'll sell it.

Not so fast. You're not the only game in town. According to Larry Walsh, CEO and chief analyst of The 2112 Group, the average partner is actively engaged with four to seven brands but may have contracts to sell for as many as twenty-four to thirty-six brands, albeit opportunistically. Some of them may compete directly with you and many partners like it that way. They can present to their customers both Solution A and Solution B, covering all the bases and acquiring for themselves the perception of neutrality.

Your job, of course, is to steer them toward your solution, and that means not taking for granted that their selling world revolves around you. As discussed in Chapter 2, your partners have their own concerns and their own interests, and with other brands knocking on their doors, their attention isn't always on you.

You need to take the time to sell them on your solution. Your partners need to know what it does, the problems it solves, where they fit in the process, and their opportunity for incremental revenue, among other things.

Customer testimonials are especially useful at this stage. So are success stories, especially those backed up with robust data. Look for ways to motivate your partners to buy in. Leverage

FOMO where you can—the Fear of Missing Out. Once you have a few partners winning with you, more partners will climb aboard.

A final note: In our discussion with brands, we've learned that partners are becoming increasingly sophisticated when it comes to assessing the revenue and profit for a given product line. Our advice is to anticipate this. Don't take anything for granted, but also know that the partners that do buy-in will be more committed and probably more successful.

To-Partner: Recommending (Delighting)

A successful buyer's journey ends in the recommending stage. This is our buyer-centric model, and it's essential when considering end-users. Your partners may not be using your product or service but they are using your tools, research, best practices, communications, testimonials, and everything else you provide them to understand the market, learn about what you offer, and buy into the idea of selling your solutions.

Not that they're prohibited from recommending your partner program, but it's not realistic to assume your partners are going to help you recruit other partners. It happens, of course. Sometimes, for example, with a disruptive product in a newly discovered market, a concerted effort by a lot of different people can help publicize it, and everybody wins. More partners lead to more activity all around and, at least at first, there's enough business to go around. More likely, however, your partners aren't interested in educating others who might turn in to competitors. It's more appropriate, therefore, to return to Halligan and Shah's term here of "delight" to more accurately define the goal at this final stage of the to-partner marketing process.

At this point, you want your partners to be delighted with your partner program, and you want them to remain that way. Delighting is often overlooked by brands who think that the end of the journey is to get the partner transacting. Keep them happy and keep them selling!

It's important to consider that while everybody wants to get their partners to this stage, there's no shortcut for it. You can't just skip over everything that comes before.

No matter how effective your partners are in selling your product or service, you can never take for granted that they'll diligently keep at it. There's not a thing in the universe that doesn't eventually run out of steam, your partners' efforts included. They slow down. They get stuck. Your job is to energize, excite, and unstick them.

Unsticking your partners might be a matter of anticipating their problems so you can give them the tools and resources they need to overcome. Problems are inevitable. Potential end-users voice objections, they question the value, they consider the alternatives from the competition. If you can *proactively* address the points of friction in the transaction process, you'll go a long way in keeping your partners happy.

Keeping them Motivated

You should give rewards and recognition, too, but not just to the partner organization. *The most effective incentive programs target the individual sales rep, not the company.* Further to this point, we've seen many companies make the mistake of paying an incentive on the transaction and this is a waste. The sales rep is already earning a commission. An evolved incentive strategy is one where you provide incentives for the *behaviors* that lead to a transaction. Think of the marketing, sales, and training activities that are necessary for a transaction to take place, and reward a partner sales rep for achieving them.

Rewards don't have to be huge. Almost everyone appreciates gratitude, even a token of it. It's incredible what a ten-dollar Starbucks card can do for loyalty.

Partner sales reps are inherently competitive. You may think a gift card is hardly worth anyone's time, but consider this: Often, it's not about the gift card; it's about winning.

To-partner marketing is often overlooked. Partners are always there, so why should you need to keep selling them? For the same reason you nurture any relationship: To keep it healthy, vibrant, and *working*.

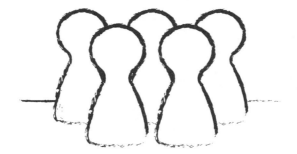

FIVE

WITH, THROUGH AND FOR PARTNER MARKETING

In to-partner marketing, we regard the partner as a customer. The orientation of our approach changes when we market *with* or *through* or *for* our partners. In each of these cases, the customer is the end user of our products or services and the partner has a role in delivering the message.

In many cases, the partner's natural inclination is to skip over the *learning* phase of the buyer's journey. They want to rush right over the teaching and get to the sale but this doesn't work. Buyers need to learn first. The role of the brand is to create rich content to help prospects learn and to make it available to partners to execute. It's equally important that brands coach their partners on how to use this top-of-the-funnel content when delivering it to the market.

The role of the channel partner is to use the learning content provided by the brand to educate prospective buyers and create teaching moments that build engagement and interest in the products and solutions.

Whether you are marketing with, through, or for your partners, several proven tactics can help attract prospects and then progress them through the *learning, shopping, buying,* and *recommending* stages. Samples of each of these tactics are available at our website: *http://www.marketingmultiplied-book. com.*

Learning

Recall that in the *learning* phase, the potential buyer is a buyer in theory only. They're not looking at your solution, or anybody's solution, because they don't yet recognize there's a problem that needs to be solved. But like all of us, they're soaking in information every day that comes from a wide variety of sources. To make a meaningful connection, you and your partners must be positioned as a credible source of information. Tactically, this will take several forms.

Videos

Content in the form of video educates potential prospects about the pain they might be experiencing and provides information on what you and your partners have learned about solving these problems.

Our take: Videos are a terrific way to bring awareness to a problem and they're most effective when brief, specific, and eye-catching. They're especially useful in short-form. You've seen them as you've scrolled through your social media feed. The most effective videos have subtitles and capture your attention in the first few seconds.

How important is video becoming? According to a recent report, eighty-five percent of businesses now have internal staff and resources producing videos in-house.[11] Why? Because over *twenty billion videos a day are* viewed on Facebook, Snapchat, and YouTube alone.[12]

Over twenty billion videos a day are viewed on Facebook, Snapchat, and YouTube alone.

---

[11]   2017 Video in Business Benchmark Report by Vidyard.

[12]   Ibid

When we see video in the channel, it's often brand-centric. While this is good for the brand, it's not especially useful for the partner. It's a common misconception that a video must be professionally produced (read: expensive), which would preclude most partners from leveraging this tactic. It's not true; content and authenticity are far more critical than production value. Our recommendation is to provide video-creation best practices, scripts, and ideas to your partners. Videos can be recorded on their mobile devices or their desktop cameras, and products like Camtasia make it easy for almost anyone to produce a finished piece of video content.

Further, emerging companies like Vidyard have built video personalizing engines, where information about the viewer is embedded in the video. Prospects are always delighted to see their name or company show up in a promotional video and the open, click-through, and viewing rates are significantly higher than generic videos.

A key frame from a video personalized to the prospect

Infographics

These are interesting and informative visuals that talk to buyers' pains using statistics and facts to drive interest.

Our take: Infographics can take complex subjects and present them in a way that makes them understandable. The most useful infographics are easy for people to digest and just as easy to share. Not everything you present is going to go viral, of course, but creating something that's worth tweeting and retweeting can help spread an idea at a low cost. Infographics can be compelling in and of themselves, or they can also be used as teasers to drive people to longer-form content like blogs or eBooks.

When creating infographics, leave room for your partners' logo and messaging to ensure it can be easily co-branded.

A co-branded infographic

eBooks

These are short-form electronic books that speak to a pain and potential solution, or perhaps a possible opportunity.

Our take: eBooks often validate an idea that a potential consumer might have, either for herself or for others she might need to convince. Maybe she's contemplating a problem but can't get others within her organization to see it. A well-written eBook with quantitative information can help her make a case. It's a portable and easy-to-share way to display relevant content.

To make eBooks work in your channel, consider leaving a placeholder to allow your partners to write the copy for the introductory page, and to co-brand it.

Launch Communication Plan eBook

When launching a new program or platform to increase channel partner engagement, using a communication plan that both educates and motivates partners to use your tool or program will increase your chances for engagement after launch.

The cover and description for an eBook

Blogs

Blog articles should focus on one topic and be somewhere between 400 and 600 words in length.

Our take: An excellent blog, like an infographic, can be compelling on its own in presenting a pain or an opportunity, or at directing a potential customer elsewhere with a call to action—a link, for instance, to a more in-depth eBook. Blog articles should be made available to partners in an easy to copy and paste format so they can use them on their blogs. We also recommend putting together a blogging how-to and best practices guide for your partners.

Pulling it all together

The best practice is to package these in a single bill of materials, so partners can deliver an integrated set of learning assets to prospects. For example, the partner would take your blog article and customize it by adding some of their thoughts to the starter you've given them and then integrate a video or infographic to break up the content, with the eBook as a call to action. Promoting that blog article through social media and email will help reach their prospects wherever they're looking for information.

Additional Thoughts on Content

Your content should be aligned to present a central idea to people who have different learning styles and different attention spans. A visually-oriented person may prefer soaking in his information from a video or graphic, while others will peruse a blog. An eBook will appeal to someone who's seeking more detail. You need to position your partners to be in front of their future customer in whatever way that customer learns best.

A not-so-minor benefit: while these tactics tell your story to your prospective buyer, they tell search engines too. This is true for your partners as well; when they embed your content on their website, it establishes a connection between your brand and theirs as far as search engine indexes are concerned. For relevant keyword searches, their ranking will rise over time.

Copy blocks can also be handy for your partners. These are specific messages that partners can create their content around, and they should just be a paragraph or two—a key piece of information, even a statistic or a reference to a recent study that highlights a relevant problem or opportunity.

Social media copy blocks, like pre-written LinkedIn posts, Tweets, or Facebook messages, can be used to drive people to additional content. Give your partners copy blocks they can use to attract the attention of potential customers.

Social Media Copy
SAP SuccessFactors Recruiting – Sample Tweets

Imagine if you could hire the very best people on the planet? You can. And we'll help you find them. #SAPSuccessFactors Recruiting

Even with great products, great business models, great strategy, great everything—you need a great workforce to make it all happen. #SAPSuccessFactors Recruiting

The end-to-end, step-by-step tool for sourcing, engaging and hiring top talent. Because your people are your ONE indispensable asset. #SAPSuccessFactors Recruiting

Sample social media copy blocks

Writing is Hard

A note about writing: partners usually don't love to do this. It's difficult, time-consuming, and, let's face it, what they write may not even accurately describe your products or their benefits.

And yet, as we've explained, content is critical in establishing domain expertise and displaying thought leadership. We know it's a lot of work but provide as much content as you can to your partners, in whatever form you can. Not only will your work be appreciated, but it will also allow you to synchronize your message in the marketplace.

Finally, keep in mind that the tactics we've described above are aligned to the *learning* stage of the buyer's journey, where the goal is to build awareness about pain or opportunity, delivered from the partner. It should be devoid of product mention, as it's too early and will be a waste of marketing effort. Save the product-focused content for later.

To Brand or Co-Brand

Co-branding refers to your logo and the partner's logo on a web page, eBook, or other marketing materials. In many cases they will be treated as equals; they'll be the same size and share the same prominence on the asset. This is the recommended best practice. Co-branding is helpful to the partner because of the credibility your brand brings to them.

There's no reason your content, in whatever form it takes, can't be co-branded. Even videos can be customized with your partner's name and logo. This can make a powerful statement for partners who might otherwise not have the budget or expertise to produce their own videos.

When deciding whether to co-brand materials, the critical question to ask is this: will it help the partner, hurt the partner, or have no effect if your brand is locked up next to theirs on this content? How do the partner's customers perceive your solution? You might be an ingredient brand for a partner who's using your product as one component among many in their solution. Your brand–and your logo–might mean very little to the end-user. On the other hand, your brand may be highly recognizable and your partner may benefit by sharing the logo space. Co-branding can be a big win for your partners, making an impact they could not get on their own.

Deciding how much of a halo effect you can provide your partners requires an honest assessment. No doubt you're proud of your brand—and you should be. Still, will your logo make a difference with the typical customer of your partner? That's what matters.

Shopping

All the same tactics can be used for a buyer in *shopping* mode but the approach changes. Now the prospect has gained some awareness of a problem or the opportunity, so it's time to reveal your solution as you market with, through, and for your partners.

Videos, infographics, eBooks, and blogs can all help your partners educate a buyer who is now considering taking the next step in the journey. She's got a problem and she's aware of it. How has your solution helped others who have had the same problem, and how have your partners helped with that? This is now the orientation across the various modes of content delivery.

Be careful not to encroach on content that is oriented towards buying! The prospect isn't there yet and it's too early for your partner to try to close the deal. At this point, your goal is to acquaint the potential customer with your solution and the value your partner provides, not to relay why yours is the best solution out of the several that might be available.

In with-partner and for-partner marketing, you'll be very descriptive and specific with your content. Your joint-marketing goals are mostly the same. But in your through-partner efforts, you might need to be more generic and allow some flexibility in your content to give the partner space to put their unique spin on it. The key is to contextualize your content: are you reaching the prospect in shopping mode *with* your partner, *through* your partner, or *for* your partner? Your approach will differ for each avenue.

Shopping content is about informing and educating people about your solution and their opportunity. In addition to doing so with the tactics we reviewed in the *learning* mode (now reoriented), other tactics might include:

Webinars

These are solution-oriented presentations that are typically too involved for someone in *learning* mode but are very effective in the shopping stage.

Our take: Webinars derive a lot of their effectiveness from their interactivity. People can ask questions that can be answered on the spot. That said, it's essential to make your webinars available to the prospect on his or her time. Recorded webcasts that are made available for viewing through a simple registration mechanism are just as useful as live webinars. Not everybody is going to be able to make the time for the live event (meaning you shouldn't be discouraged by low attendance). Interested shoppers will be willing to take the time when it's convenient for them—later that night, at 3:00 a.m. the next morning, the following weekend, six months, or even a year later! Unless your content is rapidly changing, a good webcast can have a long shelf life.

Allowing your prospects to learn and shop on their time-table— "asynchronous" marketing—is the effective approach for today's buyer. Of course, it would be ideal to be right there with the prospect—in sync—every step of the way through the learning and shopping stages, but that's not practical, or even necessary. Making your content freely available and letting your prospects review it at their convenience makes you a helpful source of information and a more likely candidate from which your prospects will ultimately buy.

Recorded webinars are also very easy for partners to share with their prospects and customers, and when you enable them to do so, you capitalize on the multiplication effect of the channel.

Another creative use for webinars is to strip out the audio and create a podcast from it that can be delivered through iTunes, SoundCloud, and others. Camtasia is inexpensive software that allows you to export just the audio track. Now your audience can learn from you and your partners while they're in the car, at the gym, or whenever it's convenient for them.

A final note about webinars: The most effective presentations engage the audience from the start. The best way to do this is to use polls, a feature available in many popular webinar delivery platforms. Start your presentation with an interactive multiple-choice survey and then read back the results. Chances are you will already know the answer to your question and your content will be tailored to that. Intersperse other polls throughout the presentation. This simple trick will help keep your audience engaged to the end.

> Try creating a partner podcast program. Host a co-presented webinar with a partner, make it available on-demand, strip out the audio and post it on iTunes. Then provide your partners with copy for promotional emails and social media posts.

White Papers

Longer than an eBook, a typical white paper goes into detail about a specific problem, the solution, and the steps to implement the solution, all from a customer's point of view. These are typically ten to fifteen pages in length.

Our take: As with webinars, these are best when the buyer has reached a higher level of commitment than in the *learning* stage. Obviously, these are meant more for people who prefer to gather their information in the form of the written word, but that doesn't mean you don't have to pay attention to the visuals. The best white papers are clearly and intuitively outlined and contain enlightening graphics and illustrations. We're seeing a reduction in the importance of white papers these days as fewer people seem to be taking the time to read them. Nevertheless, in the spirit of catering to the buyer in the form in which the buyer shops, it's a good idea to continue to make these available.

In our experience, it is unnecessary to go to great lengths to involve a partner in the creation of a white paper. Co-branding them garners little return for the effort. However, white papers are practical as they offer content behind gated calls to action and partners appreciate this.

Web Content, Copy Blocks, and Keywords

These represent material that partners can use to showcase your solution on their website or social media stream. When a web visitor arrives on a partner's website to understand the services they offer, you want to create an opportunity for the visitor to learn about your products too.

Our take: The idea is to make it easy for your partners to deliver content about your solution to their web visitors. You might choose to provide this through a content syndication engine, or you can provide blocks of text that your partners can combine with their own writing. The keywords prevalent in the content for this stage should be aligned with shopping behavior.

Content syndication should not be simple marketing copy though. It's also an opportunity to present some of your other tactics on your partners' websites, like videos, eBooks, and infographics.

Analyst Reports

In shopping mode, buyers are frequently making comparisons between various solutions. Organizations like SiriusDecisions, Forrester Research, Gartner, The 2112 Group, and others provide analysis that can be shared with buyers through your partners.

Our take: Third-party analyst reports can be useful in substantiating your value in the marketplace. (Assuming, that is, that your product or service ranks well compared to the competition!) We've found that some companies rely too much on analyst reports, however. They can be valuable but should never replace your efforts to explain your product and its place in the market. As validation material, a favorable report should make a helpful adjunct to your content at most. Only you can tell the real story you want your prospects to hear.

Like white papers, it doesn't make sense to co-brand an analyst report but they are useful for gated offers.

Buying

Now the mindset of the prospect has shifted from shopping (an evaluation of the available solutions in the market) to buying (making a purchase). Once again, there's no reason the tactics above can't be used to help accelerate this transition. A video, blog, white paper, webcast, or analyst report might be all that's necessary to transition a shopper into a buyer. There are, however, a few tactics that are particularly effective for partners to leverage in the buying stage.

Case Studies

A testimonial from a customer, whether delivered live, via video, or in written form, can be extraordinarily powerful in the buying stage.

Our take: The buying stage produces a natural moment of doubt for anyone poised to make a significant purchase. If you think back to when you purchased your last car, you probably remember how this moment feels. A well-timed peer-to-peer testimonial can provide the psychological affirmation a prospect needs.

Keep in mind your channel partners might not have testimonials of their own and likely won't know how to write an effective case study. In our experience, it's best to partner with an agency that has writers on staff and relevant expertise.

Seminars

Seminars allow a partner and prospect to come face-to-face. What the prospect wants to do is look the partner in the eye and feel confident that he's about to make the right choice.

Our take: An in-person event provides an excellent opportunity to present customer testimonials. Nothing reaffirms a decision quite like a live speaker telling a "how this solution helped me" story. Additional material that can be covered live and in-person might include a product review, demonstration, or case study.

The most effective way to do this is to invite existing customers and mix-in prospects that are in the buying stage. The result is an in-person case study. You and your partners are allowing the prospect to meet the future version of themselves, those who have already made the leap of faith and are experiencing the benefits.

Buying Guides, Pricing Guides, and ROI calculators

These are additional tools to help erase any final doubts.

Our take: A buying guide focuses on the benefits and options of your solution that the purchaser will need to choose, helping her to walk through the process smoothly and painlessly. A pricing guide describes the costs. Both will help align the buyer's vision with your deliverable, making sure they're getting what they're expecting. An ROI calculator helps substantiate the financial benefits. These can all be efficiently used for a single purchaser, or perhaps to help a purchaser make the final case to a CFO who might need a push to get on board with the decision.

Each of the assets can and should be co-branded, so a partner has a unique version to send their prospects to, or at the very least a syndicated version so that partners have these assets available on their website.

Sales Offers and Channel Incentives

Discounts, promotions, rebates, and other incentives can all be used to encourage a buyer to act. These should be included as a complement to your campaigns.

Our take: Sales offers targeted at the end user (temporary discounts or special pricing) can help provide a sense of urgency to the sale. "Buy now and save." Or even, "Buy *more* and save." Incentives delivered through your channel partners can invoke the same sense of urgency.

Often the key to offers and incentives is recognizing the potential sticking points. What are the objections that might be holding up a sale? Knowing these allows you to architect an incentive campaign that can overcome any remaining perceived risk of buying.

If you're in channel marketing, you might not be responsible for creating these types of incentives. However, given your unique position between the channel partner and your brand, you are a stakeholder in them. Too often, we see brands introduce incentives when it's too late, when marketing programs or sales results are suffering. We believe it's best to be proactive and introduce incentives with every campaign, which will accelerate sales.

Recommending

Well-placed content can influence a partners' future customers. Brands must enable their partners to help their customers share the successes they've experienced. Here are a few useful tactics:

Social Media

End-user recommendation today is mostly socially centered, so this is the most critical of all recommending tactics.

Our take: People share their stories on LinkedIn, Facebook, and Twitter. Help your partners with social media copy blocks that feature customers singing the praises of your solution. Give them content to tweet and retweet, post and re-post. Encourage them to put their unique spin on it.

Customer Events

Loyalty often precedes recommending, and breeding loyalty usually means offering rewards exclusively to customers. Offer your customers select membership in "the club," whether that means an online Facebook community, LinkedIn group, or some form of points earned by repeat purchases. People want to belong and a club is a terrific way to encourage continued interest and future recommendations.

Encourage your partners to create cohort groups of their customers and facilitate interaction on social networks. A software user group is an excellent example of a group of customers with a shared experience, and partners can play a role in facilitating the dialog and networking opportunities at these events. User groups are fun as in-person events or hosted virtually through platforms like LinkedIn Groups.

Referral programs

Want recommendations? Make it worth your customer's while.

Our take: Let's cut to the chase. Points, discounts, gift cards—reward your customers for bringing other customers. They're happy with your solution but that doesn't mean they're going to tell everyone they know. With a little incentive, however, they just might be more apt to talk about your brand.

For more on how to build effective referral programs, check out the fantastic eBook titled *The Little Black Book of B2B Referrals* by Influitive.[13]

Don't assume your partners are busy asking customers for recommendations. Frontline salespeople are typically engaged somewhere in the first three phases and mainly working with prospects in shopping or buying mode. Just as referral programs can be rolled out to end-customers, they can incorporate channel partners as well.

A final note: Timing is critical when seeking recommendations. No one wants to participate in a case study a month after buying a product, but if you wait until the customer has the chance to realize the value, they may be proud to share their experience with you.

Whether you're marketing with your partners, through your partners, or for your partners, you're limited only by your imagination. The key is in implementing the right tactics at the right time.

---

[13] A link to this eBook can be found on our website at *marketingmultiplied-book. com.*

SIX

PUTTING IT ALL TOGETHER IN A CAMPAIGN

To demonstrate how to apply these frameworks, let's overlay the modern buyer's journey and the *to*, *with*, *through* and *for* motions of channel marketing using the scenario of a brand who offers a CRM product through partners.

Learning

Since the buyer's behavior in this stage is *learning*, your role, and that of your partners, must be teaching.

Key Message/ Premise	Buyers are more likely to purchase from sales reps who take the time to use social media to research the company and the buyer
Target Buyer Personas	People who buy CRM software, e.g. sales leadership, sales operations
To-Partner Message	Companies are struggling to put social selling techniques into practice. This campaign is designed to educate prospects about the opportunities social selling can open for them and the products that enable it.
	As our partner, we think there's an opportunity for you to help educate buyers about this need and tell the story that, later in the journey, makes the case for your products and services.
With-Partner Message	Deliver a blog article or other content to the partner that makes the case for social selling and how buyers respond better to sales reps that leverage social information.
	Since this message will go to market with the brand and the partner, we'll include an example from both participants on successful social selling and why it matters.

Key Message/ Premise	Buyers are more likely to purchase from sales reps who take the time to use social media to research the company and the buyer
Through-Partner Message	Like the with-partner motion, deliver a blog article or other content to the partner that they can use to make the case for social selling and how buyers respond better to sales reps that leverage social information.
	Each partner should personalize the brand's content with a story from their practice. Ideally, this will be from their personal experience, e.g. "We found social selling to be beneficial..." Assets should be co-branded.
For-Partner Message	The brand should personalize the learning content with a different social selling example for each partner, e.g. Partner A example is different than Partner B example.
Tools and Tactics to Execute Message	Blogging Video Social media

Shopping

As prospects progress from *learning* to *shopping*, it's time to present them with content that describes the capabilities offered by you and your partners.

Key Message/ Premise	CRM software makes it easy for sales reps to acquire social media information about companies and specific buyers
Target Buyer Personas	People who buy CRM software, e.g. sales leadership, sales operations

Key Message/ Premise	CRM software makes it easy for sales reps to acquire social media information about companies and specific buyers
To-Partner Message	The brand shares information with the partners about the market opportunity for CRM software and how social selling capabilities are driving buyer interest. How many customers are targets for this? Which industries? Size of deals expected?
With-Partner Message	Develop solution-oriented content that describes the product offered and integrates information about the partner's *solution*. The call to action should move the prospect from shopping to buying, typically with some sort of product trial, *assisted by the partner*.
Through-Partner Message	Develop solution-oriented content that describes the product offered and integrates information about the partner's *value-added services*. The call to action should move the prospect from shopping to buying, typically with some sort of product trial, *assisted by the partner*.
For-Partner Message	Develop solution-oriented content that describes the product offered and integrates information about the partner's *solution or value-added services*. The call to action should move the prospect from shopping to buying, typically with some sort of product trial, *assisted by the brand*.
Tools and Tactics to Execute Message	Webinars Landing pages (e.g. software trials, eBooks, white papers)

Buying

In the buying stage, it's time to prove that you and your partners are worthy of the customer's trust.

Key Message/ Premise	Our CRM software is the best solution available on the market to enable social selling. Companies who choose this solution will achieve impressive results.
Target Buyer Personas	People who buy CRM software, e.g. sales leadership, sales operations
To-Partner Message	It's time to make the case for why partners should sell/service your CRM product among all the other choices available in the market. How will the partner make more money, develop deeper customer relationships and earn great profits? Whatever makes your solution unique in the market, now is the time to make your case to partners. Don't take it for granted that they know it.
With-Partner Message	Among all the choices in the market, why is the solution presented by you and your partner the right one for the customer? The case you make should include a compelling message that combines the brand and partner value propositions. Ideally, you'll use real examples of companies who have successfully adopted your solution and realized the benefits presented in the shopping content presented previously. If the partner has specific customer examples, those would be best, rather than case studies unrelated to this specific partner. It's important at this stage to impress upon the prospect how *you and the partner will work together* to ensure success.

Key Message/ Premise	Our CRM software is the best solution available on the market to enable social selling. Companies who choose this solution will achieve impressive results.
Through-Partner Message	Among all the choices in the market, why is the solution presented by you and your partner the right one for the customer? The case you make should include a compelling message that combines the brand and partner value propositions. Ideally, you'll use real examples of companies who have successfully adopted your solution and realized the benefits presented in the shopping content presented previously. If the partner has specific customer examples, those would be best, rather than case studies unrelated to this specific partner. It's important at this stage to impress upon the prospect how the partner will work to ensure their success with support from you.
For-Partner Message	Among all the choices in the market, why is the solution presented by you and your partner the right one for the customer? The case you make should include a compelling message that combines the brand and partner value propositions. Ideally, you'll use real examples of companies who have successfully adopted your solution and realized the benefits presented in the shopping content presented previously. If the partner has specific customer examples, those would be best, rather than case studies unrelated to this specific partner. It's important at this stage to impress upon the prospect how the partner will work to ensure their success with support from you.
Tools and Tactics to Execute Message	Email Case studies Seminars/ In-person events Buying guides

Recommending

Recommending is the fourth and final stage and it enables partners and customers to celebrate their success. The benefit to you is that they influence others, your future prospects.

Key Message/ Premise	Post-purchase information to help get the most out of the commitment made to the CRM software. Create a great customer experience and recommendations will follow.
Target Buyer Personas	People who have purchased your CRM software, e.g. sales leadership, sales operations
To-Partner Message	Having partners provide testimonials to other partners can be quite powerful in your partner recruitment and activation plans. That's the main value to you. So, what's in it for them? Partners enjoy attention that recognizes their expertise, their business sense, and their ability to deliver great customer experiences. Use these factors in your to-partner message to encourage them to recommend your product to other partners.
With-Partner Message	The customer is enjoying the benefits that they expected from the product or service they purchased. Share content that gently encourages customers to share their satisfaction with others, highlighting both the brand and the partner.
Through-Partner Message	The customer is enjoying the benefits that they expected from the product or service they purchased. Provide your partners with content that gently encourages customers to share their satisfaction with others, highlighting both the brand and the partner.
For-Partner Message	The customer is enjoying the benefits that they expected from the product or service they purchased. Share content that gently encourages customers to share their satisfaction with others, highlighting both the brand and the partner.

Key Message/ Premise	Post-purchase information to help get the most out of the commitment made to the CRM software. Create a great customer experience and recommendations will follow.
Tools and Tactics to Execute Message	Social media Email Customer events Referral programs

The Full Campaign Plan

As you plan the campaigns and programs you'll develop for your partners, we recommend using the table below to lay out all your messages side by side. In doing so, you can plan how you'll progress your partners and prospects through the buyer's journey with the unique messages suited to each stage. Use the template below and fill in the blanks.[14]

	Learning	Shopping	Buying	Recommending
Key Message/ Premise				
Target Buyer Personas				
To-Partner Message				
With-Partner Message				

---

[14]   This template can also be found on our website at *marketingmultiplied-book.com.*

	Learning	Shopping	Buying	Recommending
Through-Partner Message				
For-Partner Message				
Tools and Tactics to Execute Message				

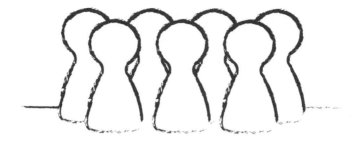

CHANNEL MARKETING MATURITY MODEL

We've spent a lot of time describing to, with, through, and for-partner marketing but how is a channel marketer supposed to know which motion to use, and when?

We developed a model to help you determine just how much (or little) marketing support an individual partner needs. In each engagement mode, there are inflection points, or partner behaviors, that indicate the partner is ready to move to the next mode. No matter how mature your partner marketing program is, all partners must walk with you before they run.

CHANNEL MARKETING MATURITY MODEL

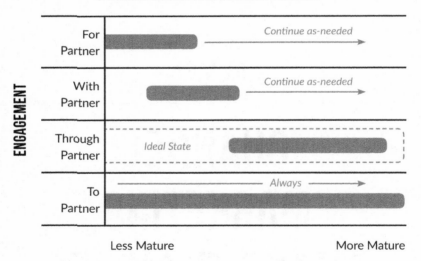

For-partner marketing is where we start. It's for new partners that are just becoming familiar with your partner program benefits. You want to make a good impression, and for-partner marketing is a show of goodwill on your part. For-partner marketing is also appropriate for partners with less credibility in the market, and those that will benefit from the halo effect of your brand.

Alternatively, you may present this opportunity to top-performing partners, where you want to capture mindshare by offering them a turnkey marketing experience, or for larger partners, where to get their attention you'll have to do the work for them.

Once you get a few for-partner initiatives under your belt, you'll want to graduate your partners to a with-partner engagement model, continuing to do for-partner marketing on an as-needed or occasional basis.

A word of caution here: Brands that don't nurture their partners to the next step of the maturity model will find themselves acting as a marketing agency for their partners, continually fielding one-off requests, and growing more resource-constrained by the day. This isn't good for anyone.

Now that the partner's confidence and abilities have grown, we switch to a **with-partner marketing** mode. The partner has the human resources to deliver a joint message and, more importantly, they have a "better-together" story to tell. As a brand, you have a strong incentive to participate in these types of activities; you'll want to be present to deliver the message and to gain access to the partner's customers.

Finally, we arrive at the **through-partner marketing** mode, which is the ideal state. At this point, the partner has demonstrated proficiency in carrying your message to the market and a willingness (and the resources) to execute marketing campaigns on your behalf. This is where you begin to enjoy the multiplying effect of the channel because, in this mode, you create the content once and your partners execute it repeatedly to different audiences.

As we described in Chapter 4, the **to-partner marketing** efforts should be continuous. Help your partner build skills and stay top of mind, no matter how long they've been in your program.

Of the first three modes, it will be helpful to plot your partners on each continuum, which will reveal the type of support they need from you. For each partner, ask yourself the following questions and apply a score of 1 to 3, with one being least robust and 3 being most robust:

- How long have they been in our partner program?

- What is their annual revenue with us? What does that look like in the context of their overall business?

- How much is our brand a part of their overall business?

- How many marketing resources do they have on staff?

- What is their market presence? Things to consider are their website and their social media presence and activity. How established and known are they in their market?

A score between 5 and 8 puts the partner squarely in the for-partner mode. They need a lot of help from you. Between 9 and 12 and they're ready for a with-partner engagement, where the 1+1 story is strong. A score of 13 or higher and they're off and running, so target your through-partner activities at them.

For larger channels, it may be the channel account manager (CAM) that will be the best person to perform this assessment. We've created a worksheet available in the Resources section of our website that you can adapt and distribute accordingly. Once the CAMs have completed the assessments, gather the results and see what segments of partners you can develop and create programs that will suit their needs and abilities.

Finally, it's important to note that the Channel Marketing Maturity Model applies to your partners, not your company. It has nothing to do with how mature your organization is; we've seen brands with $2 billion-plus in annual revenue that have an entirely for-partner engagement model. Our advice is to evaluate each partner and then select an engagement mode that's appropriate for their level of maturity.

One caveat: For some channels, it will never be appropriate to graduate partners from one stage to the next. We're thinking about referral programs here. These types of channel partners are not waking up thinking about the brand and likely won't ever be in a through-partner mode. They still have access to an audience that the brand will find enticing, and so a for-partner and with-partner mode will always make sense for them.

In any case, knowing how to support your partners starts with the understanding of where they are.

EIGHT

THE CHANNEL ENGAGEMENT FRAMEWORK

We've covered a lot of ground at a conceptual level and now it's time to put it into practice. To do this effectively you'll need a system. Your efforts should revolve around the *channel engagement framework*.

We developed this framework to help you systematize your channel execution, to drive alignment and set expectations for all parties involved. This model is simple and adaptable and it covers six essential steps:

- Planning
- Enablement
- Communication
- Demand Creation
- Evangelism
- Measurement

We'll consider these one at a time. Your commitment to this practical framework can make the difference between efficient channel execution that partners understand and are onboard with, and an ineffective implementation that does more harm than good.

"If you fail to plan, you are planning to fail!"

–BENJAMIN FRANKLIN

It All Starts with a Plan

Planning is the essential first step in the channel engagement framework and there are two levels to it. The first is an internal exercise—developing an overall plan of what you want to accomplish with your partners. The second is external, developing partner-specific plans with a standard set of goals that you and your channel partners agree to pursue.

Depending on the size of your channel, it might not be practical to create specific plans with every partner, but you probably know some of the partners you can collaborate and strategize with to generate workable plans and goals. We find most organizations rely on the 80/20 "Pareto" principle—that is, 80 percent of their business comes from 20 percent of their partners. This 20 percent is where most of your planning will probably occur.

It is an accepted fact that partners with marketing plans perform better than partners without. Planning with your partner can be as simple as putting together some notes on a cocktail napkin. Better planning follows a methodology like the one described here. The key is to document your shared goals in writing, which gives you and your partner something tangible for use with your respective teams, and a way to hold each other accountable. It's important not to complicate the process. Avoid asking partners to fill out comprehensive business plans spanning several pages.[15] If planning is too laborious or complicated, your partners aren't going to complete it, or if they do, they're not likely to read it or review it ever again. Planning shouldn't be torturous.

Planning is a Two-Way Street

Planning shouldn't be one-sided. You're not going to get very far heaping mandates onto your partners. Proper planning is about sharing your vision with your partners, whether it's quarterly or annually, or an even longer period. It's not about dictating. You and your partner have shared interests, and it's with shared investments that you need their support. This is where partner-specific planning needs to take place.

Don't assume your partners intuitively understand what your vision is, or even what your shared interests are. Take the time to explain the direction you're headed and what the associated opportunities are *for them.*

Optimizing Partner Planning

To make the most of your partner planning work, we recommend the following:

---

[15] You can find a generic planning template in the Resources section of our website at *marketingmultiplied-book.com.*

- Define success by agreeing to three or four measurable outcomes that will indicate if the partnership is succeeding. For example: add twenty new customers; increase cross-sell penetration to forty-five percent; open a London sales office.

- Focus on the strategy before the tactics. Figure out *what* you are trying to accomplish before you decide *how* to accomplish it.

- Define the roles and responsibilities from the outset so everyone knows what's required of them and expectations are made clear.

- Schedule a monthly or quarterly meeting with your partners and refer to the plan during the sessions to track progress and drive accountability.

Planning should be an integrated effort, with both sales and marketing at the table at the same time. Sometimes we see a sales plan with a partner and then marketing comes along later to make another plan. Integrating sales and marketing is an opportunity for efficiency.

Enablement

To achieve the goals defined in the plan, your partners will likely need some support from your company. Understanding what your partners are trying to do, and how they are trying to do it (learned during the planning process), will help you create the right mix of enablement tactics for your channel.

Enablement can take many forms. Sales collateral can help support your partners' selling efforts by relieving them of having to produce presentations and sales collateral. Marketing materials can enable through-partner demand generation using co-branded campaign landing pages, emails, and more.

Enablement can also take the form of training—and we don't just mean product training. The value of product training speaks for itself but the most successful brands offer training in other areas too. Many channel partners need help improving their business skills, for example. Many resellers have strong technical backgrounds but lack business acumen. Learning basic business skills can be of great benefit to them. Consider partnering with an author or local business school to present a course for your partners.

Selling Skills

Your partners might need help sharpening their selling skills. You might consider providing access to external pre- and post-sales experts. Webinars are especially useful for this type of training. Topics can include how to handle objections, how to get past the gatekeeper, how to recognize opportunities, and how to close deals. You should bring in experts on social selling, inbound marketing, and customer service. We've seen some companies invite authors in to speak to their teams and many will do it at no charge in exchange for the opportunity to promote their book.

Some brands resist helping to foster this kind of development for their partners, believing it too costly or, as we mentioned in Chapter 4, not wanting to assist their partners with skills that they may use to sell other products but this is precisely *why* you should do it. Let the other brands resist helping their partners with ancillary training. Providing this kind of developmental support is a big way to differentiate your partner program.

Moreover, it doesn't have to be time-consuming and expensive. There are peer group organizations that you can recommend to your partners and programs that are available that facilitate learning among groups that share the same problems and interests. One favorite of ours is HTG[16].

Communication

Properly communicating with your channel partners is critical. Sharing ongoing updates with your partners and hearing from them regarding their needs helps to build trust in the relationship and it keeps you top-of-mind. Tailoring your communication by role is the best approach (e.g., executive, sales, marketing, technical, etc.).

The message is important but every bit as essential is the medium. Our recommendation? Video, video, video. Very few of your partners are going to read your monthly newsletter. Make it a video. Make it short and to the point and no longer than a minute or two. As we mentioned in earlier chapters, it doesn't have to be expensively produced, but it does need to offer something of value. Partners will take the time to watch if the information provides something useful and pertinent. Again, we turn to our friends at Vidyard for this. They offer a tool called GoVideo which is 100 percent free and allows anyone with a browser and a webcam to record, share, and track a video. It's a simple and elegant solution.

---

[16] *htgpeergroups.com*

Live webcasts are also a productive avenue of communication and one that encourages spontaneous interaction. Have an appealing topic that will entice your partners to attend and make sure there's plenty of opportunity for Q&A. Topics that are sure to garner partner interest are "Coming Soon" or news that has not been made public yet, promotions, and product launches. They always want to be in the know. Partners also appreciate hearing from your top executives on the direction of the business and industry trends.

Whether it's recorded video or a live webcast, it helps to make the presentation a little unpredictable so that it's not the same routine every time. Try featuring a successful partner in your videos, or interview one for the webcast. People not only derive value from a repeatable success story, they wonder how they can be the next one featured! It becomes an elite reward.

FOMO

Featuring a partner is an excellent way to instill FOMO in your channel—the Fear of Missing Out—and it's a great way to get your partners to pay attention to you. Does FOMO work? Consider the lines that people form to be the first users of a new Apple iPhone. They're not lining up for the phone's features. They may not even know what they are! They're lining up because they don't want to miss out on something new.

You can use this phenomenon to motivate your partners, not by offering the new iPhone (though that could work, too) but instead by encouraging peer envy to spur action. Partners in your channel are inherently competitive and they all want recognition from you.

Taking a partner or two who exemplify the ideal partner behaviors, and publicly recognizing their efforts in front of the rest of your channel partners is the simplest way to ignite FOMO in your channel. Reward these poster children, explain how they earned your adoration, and share their story. Let your partners know you'll be recognizing future partner success stories and encourage them to contact you with stories of their own.

One caveat: the "ideal partner behaviors" you want to show off must be achievable by the masses or this strategy will backfire. If you always recognize your most prominent and best partners, your midsize and small partners won't even try to compete.

Another way to ensure active communication by employing FOMO is to create exclusive opportunities that will benefit only those who follow your guidance. Reward your partners for paying attention, in other words. One example is to announce that on a specific date you'll be switching your Twitter handle to "Private" mode for a big announcement. On that day, only your Twitter followers will be able to read your tweets, as opposed to the public. Once private, you can make your announcement and give your dedicated followers a jump on the competition. Of course, the announcement must be something of substance, like a new price discount promotion that your partners can offer their customers, or a new event kit full of swag that's available to the first fifty partners to schedule an event focused on a specific campaign. The opportunity to have breakfast with your CEO or another executive at your next partner conference may also be enticing. We'll revisit FOMO later.

Be creative. Experiment. Just do *something*. Keep the lines of communication between you and your partners open and active.

Demand Creation

Helping your partners drive demand for your solutions is through-partner marketing and perhaps the most crucial piece of your channel execution. A good deal of this book is about demand generation, so we won't elaborate here beyond conveying its importance to your channel engagement framework. You know what you need to do!

Evangelism

Ultimately, you want your partners to act as evangelists for your company and its principal marketing messages. Generating awareness may not lead immediately or directly to revenue for you, or for them, but having your partners act as evangelists will help others become aware of your company and that awareness *will* eventually lead to the consideration of your solutions.

Here are a few ideas to propose to your partners:

- **Social media.** Tweet, share, and post in support of your marketing messages and specific campaign calls-to-action. There are tools available to help you and your partners synchronize your social posts.

- **Industry events.** Partners should be encouraged to present at industry events and other tradeshows. Build pre-packaged topics and presentations for them. The goal is to get partners on stages large and small, telling your story.

- **Industry websites and magazines.** Create blog posts and articles and submit the content to industry websites and publications with links back to the partner website, or to your site, to drive engagement with content and calls-to-action.

- **FOMO Programs.** The same fear of missing out that can keep the lines of communication open between you, and your partners can also be employed to promote evangelism. Try creating a cohort group that partners become members of based on a certain level of success (the "Winners Circle"). Give partners a reason to feel proud of the work you're doing together. Grant members early access to information, give them opportunities to speak at events, quote them in articles and blogs. If you can deepen your relationship with partners that already like you, you'll generate even more engagement.

Measurement

It's not enough to plan, enable, communicate, generate demand, and evangelize. To be successful, the outcomes of your channel engagement framework need to be measurable (and actively measured!). Are you hitting the goals of your plan? How many partners have you been able to reach with your enablement programs? With your webcasts? How many sales opportunities have you been able to generate with any given campaign? How many partners have become members of your cohort group? You'll want to measure results and you'll want to measure the behaviors that lead to the results. We'll cover metrics in greater detail in Chapter 10.

A robust channel engagement framework will help you not only systematize and organize your channel execution, but it will also help you understand the value you're driving and identify opportunities for improvement. Keep it simple, yet comprehensive. Make it flexible and make it measurable. With a proper channel engagement framework, you'll have all the pieces in place for successful channel execution.

GETTING PARTNERS TO ENGAGE

You've done all the work. Everything is in place. You've created great content. You've produced videos and battle cards, infographics, and social media copy blocks. You've even invested in a partner portal, partner marketing engine, a learning management system—everything your partners need to succeed with your product. In short, you've built a Ferrari that's all gassed up and ready to go.

And it sits idle in the driveway.

Your partners are not taking advantage of your program benefits. Heck, you're not even sure they've noticed. Nothing is happening! You've worked so hard; how can this be?

Let's cut right to the chase: For every program you create, and every new offer you present, your partner's response is '*So what? Who cares?*'

And as much as that sucks, it's also true.

Your first obstacle to adoption is apathy. As we discussed earlier, partners are only going to move to avoid pain or if they perceive gain. It's not enough to tell them what the benefit is to them if they participate; you must articulate the next-level benefit to them (what that means to them), too.

Here's how you might articulate some of the value of a sample program to our partners:

Component	Benefit	What that means for you
Training	The development of a better understanding of the buyer's psychology.	Improvement of your sales and marketing skills.
Demand Generation Materials	Beautiful creative assets with compelling calls to action.	The ability to drive more leads for your business.

Component	Benefit	What that means for you
Sales Resources	Research, tools, competitive positioning, and objection handling.	Being positioned to drive effective sales results. Closing bigger deals, faster.
Incentives (MDF or other)	Access to funding that allows you to engage qualified agencies.	An agency helps you drive demand, and you stay focused on closing deals.

If you don't list the benefits (and the next-level benefits), you're leaving it to your partners to come to their own conclusions about your program, and those may be wrong. It's worth stating again: your partners are not waking up each morning thinking about your company and your products. You are *not* the center of their world. Just because you've built it doesn't mean they'll come.

If this is not a problem for you today, rest assured that at some point it will be. Whether a partner is new to your channel and still coming up to speed, or you have a mature relationship with a partner who is being pulled in other directions, the underlying reality of all your partner relationships is that your partners will never care about your company as much as you do.

But there are ways to make your partners pay attention, and there are ways to get them to engage. It starts with understanding that when it comes to marketing your products and solutions, there are three questions every partner has:

1. What's in it for me?

2. Who's going to pay for it?

3. Who's going to do the work?

What's in It for Them?

To answer this is to think about motivation. What's the incentive for your partners to engage? Or, to put it more pointedly, how can you incentivize your partner?

There are three primary stages of partner engagement: *learning, creating,* and *sharing.* The *learning* stage is obvious; they're trying to understand what it is you're offering. At the *creating* step, they're taking your content and doing something useful with it. At *sharing,* they're communicating your content to others. Incentives should be aligned to each stage, and by spreading incentives out, you'll be motivating your partners to put one foot in front of the other.

Incentivizing learning can be as trivial as a Starbucks card sent to every partner who attends a webcast. Maybe you're launching a new program and you need your partners to pay attention. The program will undoubtedly benefit them in the long run, but how can you get them to take the time to listen to you, just for an hour? Often that free cup of coffee or Amazon gift card is enough. Don't underestimate the value of swag—coffee mugs, t-shirts, pen sets. Even if it's small, partners appreciate you giving them something in return for their time. Make it easy on yourself and plan for convenience. Gift cards are useful because you can deliver them digitally. There's no need to order a crate of gifts that then must be broken down and shipped out in smaller boxes to each partner; you have better things to do with your time.

These are small stakes when you consider the organizational hours and resources that you put into designing programs and creating content. Remember: all you're looking to do is buy a short span of your partner's attention. It doesn't matter how valuable your new program is until it becomes valuable in your partner's eyes.

Incentive Value Deepens with Engagement

Incentives ought to become more significant with each stage of partner engagement. At the *create* and *share* stages, you're going to want to reward your partners for taking the initiative to launch marketing campaigns based on your content and reward them again when that campaign is launched to a considerable number of prospects. Keep in mind that partners will naturally follow the path of least resistance. Their interest is in spending time with customers and they're not necessarily going to jump at the chance to do the work required to find new customers. They'll be happy to let you worry about generating leads for them. Getting partners to think and act differently requires cleverness.

A gift card is useful at the *creating* and *sharing* stage but we'd encourage you to think about incentives that will drive behavior over an extended period. Raffles and contests work well for this purpose. Every time a partner creates and shares a campaign from your program, they get entered to win a trip, for example, or a chance to have breakfast with your CEO at the next conference. We talked about it in Chapter 4: rewarding for behavior rather than the transaction is far more effective in the long run. It's the repeated behavior that will result in long-term success.

Consider using a points program, with points being redeemable for various prizes.[17] Award partners points for different

---

[17]   There are many third-party companies that will help architect and deliver these types of programs. See the Resources page on our website at *marketingmultipliedbook.com*.

activities, like participating in a training activity. Executing a co-marketing activity (adding syndicated web content to their website, promoting a landing page offer, hosting an event and getting a specified number of registrants, etc.) earns them even more points.

This type of program can run for a set period or continuously. Either way, remember that the reward for selling your product—namely the profit/commission—won't be motivational for your partner in and of itself. They likely have a line of products to promote in addition to yours, each with the promise of income. Separate your programs from the start. Have an answer to the question of what's in it for them throughout the entire partner engagement process. Give your partners incentives to learn, create, and share.

Who's Going to Pay for It?

Marketing isn't cheap. The more you can help your partner financially, the higher chance your partner will engage. Co-Operational Funds (Co-op) and Market Development Funds (MDF) are common ways to supplement a partner's efforts. There are ways in which to make this funding available that consider the potential results partners will generate rather than simply looking at past sales results.

Proposal-based MDF involves funding a partner's efforts based on some form of an application process. The partner proposes a marketing initiative projecting results and you decide whether to help fund all or part of it. The problem with this approach is the obvious risk involved. The partner will invariably overstate the number of leads, opportunities, and deals they expect to gain from the activity. The agency they've chosen to help them may not align well with your brand, or be trained on the way you approach the market. The presentation the partner makes might not be effective.

But in many cases, brands choose to fund these requests anyway, with no visibility or guarantee of the ROI. They want happy partners and no one likes to say 'No'. Naturally, the partners that make funding requests receive a greater portion of the total MDF, which makes MDF allocation mostly arbitrary.

It's better to structure funding based on a partner's *earning* it, and this should not be a *percentage of revenue* or *percentage of sales projections* equation. If a partner is actively participating in all the stages of the partner engagement process—*learning, creating, sharing*—and engaging in a way that's measurable, then that's a partner that is proving worthy of an investment. They're demonstrating the right behaviors that should lead to successful transactions.

Another way to earn your support should be by displaying interest. For example, you can align the funds with the introduction of a program and limit the opportunity to a specific number of partners. Suppose you have a new lead generation program that requires the partner to have a list of contacts. You offer to provide the list for the first twenty partners that sign on to the program. There is no risk to them but only partners who are involved and paying attention are going to be able to take advantage of it.

What's important here is that the partner must do *something* apart from merely asking for funding. Attaching requirements to an MDF program is perfectly reasonable. If you have a partner that isn't willing to maintain a certain level of engagement, you're probably not very well aligned with that partner anyway. Successful partners willingly and eagerly participate.

It also helps if you can satisfactorily answer a final nagging question:

Who's Going to do the Work?

Your partners need your help, and the best support comes from a human touch. The most effective way to do this is to offer a concierge program to your partners—an actual person, or team of people, to reach out to your partners and help when it's needed. A phone call goes a lot further than a long email. Let your partners know you're there, every step of the way, ready to help, and prepared to take some of the pressure off them.

Concierge programs can be set up internally or outsourced. Many companies designate a point person or team of people to be responsible for helping their partners. Most of the time, the program starts out well, built on solid intentions. However, these initiatives frequently lose steam, falling off as the designated concierge employees, typically with already-existing company responsibilities, fall back under their regular workload. Work piles up and reaching out to partners takes a lower priority to more pressing concerns.

An external, third-party source can be much more efficient. These agencies are purpose-built for supplying the kind of daily interaction with partners that you need for a successful concierge program. They're highly specialized and can move quicker, which is paramount in an environment where partners want answers *now*. They're unrestricted by your management and corporate politics. They exist to take care of your partners and that investment is money well spent. Further, they're often less expensive than an internal hire.

They Don't Know; They Need to Be Told

Providing an answer to the three big questions that every partner has (What's in it for me? Who's going to pay for it? Who's going to do the work?) will drive your partners to engage with you throughout the entire marketing and sales process. Too often, brands consider only the last step and build their partner marketing efforts around that. There's a presupposition that your partners already know enough about your product to share it and ultimately sell it. But if they're not engaged, this is not the case. Your partners are never even going to get there until they cover the earlier steps, and walking them through those by giving them incentives will make them successful. Giving them reasons to learn, create, and share will improve the partner experience, helping you keep partners and maybe even take a few away from your competition.

Exercise

Develop a points system for various marketing activities. Provide points at each level of the *learn, create,* and *share* process. Employ a measurable benchmark for the number of points earned at each level. Use this table to outline your points program:

Marketing Activity	Learn Action	Create Action	Share Action
1.			
2.			
3.			
Incentive Earned:			

Here's a sample:

Marketing Activity	Learn Action	Create Action	Share Action
Setup Web Content Syndication	Completed training and passed quiz	Creation within marketing platform	Implementation of the code (meaning content deployed on a website)
Publish a Landing Page Offer and Promote Via Email	Completed training and passed quiz	Creation within marketing platform	Email sent to **100** contacts
Plan an Event	Completed training and passed quiz	Creation within marketing platform	**25** registered attendees
Incentive	Learn incentive: 50 points or $5?	Create incentive: 100 points or $10?	Share incentive: 500 points or $50?

TEN

MEASURE FOR SUCCESS

How do you measure success? How do you determine whether a single campaign or a series of campaigns has worked? How is your year going so far? According to plan? *Is* there a plan? If so, what's the basis of it? How do you know if you're doing a good job? Perhaps more importantly, how does your boss know you're doing a good job?

For marketers, measuring has always been problematic. A billboard advertising a soft drink goes up in a neighborhood and sales of that soft drink subsequently increase in the area. How much of the increase is due to the billboard? One hundred percent? Fifty? Can we even say with certainty that it's responsible for any of the lift?

Marketing and sales can argue about attribution all day long, despite the precision the digital world brings. Still, marketers continue to shy away from measurement. It's difficult to determine if any one sale happened because of a targeted campaign, a referral from a friend, or a single killer Tweet. And of course, measurement means accountability. Commitment to key performance indicators (KPIs) spotlights your results: you either meet the KPIs or you don't. Missed KPIs can lead to budget cuts or worse.

It gets scarier when you add partners to the mix. Partners have their own KPIs and initiatives. Just getting a partner on the phone can be a big win in some channels! Taking on a KPI that's not entirely under your control is crazy, right?

All Marketers Should Welcome Measurement

Accountability is a good thing for companies. A-players hang out with other A-players, and A-playing marketers are confident in their ability to deliver. Accountability and visibility force the lower performers into the spotlight, where they'll raise their game or go elsewhere. Either way, it's better for the company.

Further, by committing to KPIs and reporting on success, the marketing team will raise its profile with the executive team and the company. Some companies still consider marketing a luxury and, over time, positive results can shift that perception. Positive results can also reduce friction with a sales organization that may be looking down on marketers, thinking there's too much art there and not enough science. Real data can change that viewpoint, and it may also ignite discussions that increase the communication between the two organizations. Take, for instance, the age-old question "what is a qualified lead?" To some marketers, it might be someone who fills out a form on one of their web pages. To a sales rep, a qualified lead might mean a deal that closes itself. The truth is somewhere in the middle and it's different for every company. The magic happens when marketing and sales find common ground.

Measurement is good and good marketers measure. Let's consider the KPIs that channel marketers should look at when planning their campaign strategy. Let's look at goals (what you're trying to achieve), planning (how you're going to complete your goals), and metrics (how you prove you've completed them).

Set Goals

Before you launch any marketing program, you should ask yourself a fundamental question: Is there agreement across my team and organization as to what success for this program means? If not, how will you know if you can be successful? And yet, as basic as the question is, it often goes unasked. What it requires is a set of goals but this takes deep thought, which takes time, something many channel marketers don't have. Sometimes goal-setting involves a lot of guessing and, in some companies, a wrong guess can be career-limiting.

Avoiding goal-setting means never having a precise measurement of progress or success, so setting goals is a necessity. But where do you start?

Where do you fit into the Big Picture?

Since your company has probably set goals for the overall business, your job is to figure out how to contribute to those. Your concerns are different than those of your company's direct selling force, of course. Being a step removed from direct selling, you'll be focused more on activities than closing sales. Your channel partners will close. Your job is to get them up to the plate. The more at-bats, the more hits. Consequently, your goals will center on campaigns. Keep in mind, however, that not all campaigns are equal; unlike you, they're not all going to be rock stars. Your success at achieving your goals will be determined by the adjustments you make along the way.

There are many ways to set goals. The one we seem to see most often is called "prayer". We prefer the SMART method. You've probably seen this acronym before with slight variations.[18] For goal-setting success, here's the SMART way:

---

[18] The first-known use of the "S.M.A.R.T." criteria can be found in a November 1981 issue of *Management Review*: "There's a S.M.A.R.T. way to write management's goals and objectives," by George Doran.

Shared – Goals should be shared with everyone on the team. You want broad consensus.

Measurable – Metrics need to be attached, so you'll know when you've hit a goal.

Attainable – There must be at least a remote possibility that you can achieve your goals.

Relevant – Your goals need to be worthwhile and fit into the big picture.

Time-based – Every goal needs a due date.

Given this framework—knowing that whatever goals you set need to be shared, measurable, attainable, relevant, and time-based—you're ready for some specificity. If you want to do a million dollars in channel revenue, then the million-dollar question (literally) is what campaigns and activities do you launch and how many do you need to create?

Example: let's say your company has set a goal to drive $10 million in channel revenue this year. You're tasked with creating the marketing generated opportunities (MGOs) that will lead to that revenue target. Working backward, you can determine just how many you'll need to deliver. You'll want to make use of a worksheet like the one below.[19] No doubt there will be some guesswork. For example, in companies with many product lines, it's difficult to know what the average deal size is, although you could run the analysis for various segments or partner types in your channel. It's also difficult to predict

---

[19] You can download the sample worksheet from our website at *marketingmultiplied-book.com*.

how good your partners are at selling; not all partners are top performers.

Line	Measurement	% or $	Number	Formula	Description
A	Total Partners		35,000		The total number of partners enrolled in your partner program.
B	Active Partners	10%	3,500	A x B	Not all partners are engaged. This is the number of "producing" or "engaged" partners in your program.
C	Campaigns per year, per Partner		4	-	This is the number of coordinated campaign executions you want any one partner to execute in a given calendar year. If you're not sure set it to 4 (one campaign every quarter).
	Attract				
D	Responses per Campaign, per Partner		36	-	A competent partner should get at least 3 marketing responses per month, per campaign. Assume a campaign runs for 3 months.
E	Responses per Year, per Partner		144	C x D	This is the number of responses, or hand-raisers, to a campaign.
F	Response to Lead rate	10%	14	E x F	This is the percentage of responses that become leads.
	Convert				
G	Lead to Opportunity rate	25%	4	F x G	This is the percentage of leads that become opportunities.
H	Opportunities per year, total		12,600	G x B	This is the total number of Opportunities per year.
	Close				
I	Opportunity to Close/Won rate	5%	630	H x I	The percentage is the rate at which an Opportunity generated by you and delivered to the partner is closed by the partner. This number is the number of Opportunities closed per year for the channel, as a result of your marketing efforts.
J	Average deal size	$ 20,000	$ 12,600,000	I x J	This is the average size of a partner-closed deal.
K	% of revenue to partner	15%		-	This is the split to the partner for the deal.
L	Revenue to Brand		$ 10,710,000	I x (100% - K)	This is the total revenue to you, after the partner split.

The model above tells us you'll need to deliver 15,750 MGOs this year to hit a $10 million revenue target. This annual goal can then be broken down into quarterly, monthly, and even weekly targets for your team and channel partners.

Will 15,750 MGOs be enough? It's never enough! If it was, then you could do more. But you need a number to measure against that's aggressive, yet realistic and attainable. And the person best positioned to determine that number is *you*. You're the one in your organization closest to the action and you have your finger on the pulse of the channel.

Planning

Some of your insight will come from your partner planning as we discussed in Chapter 7. You know your partners and you know what percentage of them will follow through with any given campaign.

The planning process should have its own set of metrics based on channel engagement. There's one KPI that represents better than anything the true state of your channel marketing business: the percentage of partners who are *active*. Making this determination across your channel is a simple form of evaluating partner activity for the larger purpose of planning.

What does "active" mean? You might consider these two objective measures:

1. The partner organization has completed the training/enablement program you've established as a prerequisite for participation in your marketing programs.

2. The partner organization has completed at least one marketing activity; e.g., published a landing page offer, sent out a targeted email offer, or engaged a marketing agency to assist them with a campaign launch. You might also give credit to partners who download self-service assets to use in the execution of a marketing campaign.

These measures may not suit you, but the point is to have an objective KPI that you can use to efficiently make planning projections based on the level of channel engagement you can expect. This is not to suggest that you'll get zero engagement from partners that might be considered inactive by the above criteria, or that you'll get one-hundred-percent engagement from all the partners you deem active. But at least you're using an approach based on something tangible.

Whatever criteria you use, you'll want to err on the side of caution. Don't be pessimistic but not overly optimistic, either. You'll want to allow for a certain amount of failure, even from the active partners. If you conclude you need 100 activities to hit your numbers, you might consider launching 150 or 200.

Metrics

Your planning, based on partner engagement, is an ongoing process. Active/Inactive is an excellent start for making educated projections. But as your year progresses, you'll want to re-examine your level of partner engagement using real numbers and a simple model by which to do that makes use of three metrics: *reach, frequency,* and *yield.*

Reach

Reach refers to the number of partners participating in your program and it's arrived at by dividing the number of participating partners by the number of partners who are eligible to participate in your program based on whatever criteria you've established. If you have 234 out of 1,000 partner organizations participating in the program, then you have a reach of 23.4 percent. You can use this metric to set goals for your channel programs and to monitor engagement continually.

The question that often presents itself is what percentage of partners brands should expect to see participating in a program. There's no standard answer to this question. The expectations are unique to each channel. If there's no benchmark from a past program that you can use, go ahead and take your best guess and adjust as the results come in.

You may also set targets by program tier that go beyond the active/inactive dichotomy. For example, you might create a program and reasonably expect to see one hundred percent of your very top tier partners participate. You might even require their participation. For your tier two and tier three partners, you might figure a successively lower percentage.

Frequency

Frequency refers to how often your partners are participating in your program. For example, if you've asked your partners to send out a monthly email campaign to drive leads, how many partners are active each month? How many partners are participating every month? How many every other month? Every third or fourth month?

The data table for this metric would likely show what percentage of your partners sit in each bucket (number of months). Or maybe you set your target by aiming for no less than fifty percent of partners participating at least six out of twelve months.

Once you know how many partners are active in how many months, you can use this measure to identify ways to get partners to become more active. What would it take for partners who are active in two months to become active in four? You can build a specific plan to target this change and measure your progress accordingly.

Yield

Yield is the output of the channel partner activities. If the intent of your program is lead generation, how many leads are produced per partner organization? This average yield metric can be used to set targets for the entire population, for specific segments, or for individual partners.

Example: the average partner generates twenty-five leads per month in the program. If you have a group of partners who are only averaging five leads per month, what resources or programs can you offer them to help increase their yield?

Reach, frequency, and yield are valuable as individual metrics to assess program engagement, but, when combined, they become a comprehensive model.

Planning is a continuous exercise. Using your annual goals and plan, you'll be breaking things down quarterly, monthly, and weekly. Don't forget to consider seasonal factors. Certain times of the year might be slower than others and, if you run a global channel, don't forget about holidays in other parts of the world. The summer months in Europe will likely see low activity, for example. You'll want to factor in lead times, too. Don't expect a return on activities in the second quarter if your content isn't ready until a month into it.

Ultimately, the key to your success is going to be in tracking your progress *as you go* and adjusting accordingly. Moreover, for this, we need accurate, quantifiable metrics.

Example Planning Worksheet

Metrics are how you'll know when you've arrived. Here's an example of a Campaign Planning Worksheet:

Instruction	Example
Identify the overall campaign objective.	Awareness-building. Our objective is to share our point of view on channel marketing metrics and to add 120 new contacts to our database.
Set the duration of the campaign.	12 months

Instruction	Example
Identify one or more tactics you'll use to drive the campaign objective.	Our first tactic is a simple landing page with a single call to action and the offer will be an eBook on channel marketing metrics. We'll rely primarily on our social reach to drive prospects to the landing page.
Identify one or more metrics that make sense for the type of campaign you're running. • Think deeply about this! If you're running a Top of the Funnel campaign, are you likely to get a lot of marketing qualified leads from it? Probably not, because any lead you capture will most likely be discovering you for the first time, so you should pick a different KPI to measure. • Build a tracking spreadsheet and add each of the metrics to it.	Because this is a Top of the Funnel campaign, and we're going to be promoting this heavily on social media, the measurements we will capture are: 1. Social clicks, retweets, and favorites/likes/+1's 2. Landing page views 3. Net-new contacts added (eBook downloads)
Break the period into meaningful measurement points. If it's a 1-year period, break it into months. If it's a 3-year period, cut it into quarters. Then apportion your selected measurements over the same period.	As our goal is to add 120 contacts and we're running this for 12 months, we know we need to capture 10 contacts per month to hit our target.

The Roller Coaster Ride of Projects

Don't be surprised if, in the long run, your planning and goal setting follows this general pattern:

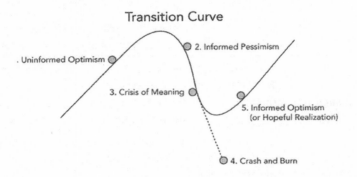

This insightful graph by Cameron Herold[20] demonstrates the transition curve of any new project.

1. We start out with Uninformed Optimism – this is going to be great and everyone will love it! I'll be a hero!

2. We move to Informed Pessimism – Hmmm, I know more than I did at the start and I see some of my short-comings. My plan was weaker than I thought and things are not going well.

3. We're now at the inflection point; the Crisis of Meaning – Have I been wrong from the beginning? What am I going to do now?

4. And it's here that we Crash and Burn, or we make the necessary adjustments and enter Informed Optimism

---

[20] *Double Double: How to Double Your Revenue and Profit in 3 Years or Less*, Cameron Herold, Greenleaf Book Group, 2011.

— I know how to do this, repeatedly, to get the results I need, and I have the metrics to prove it. "I think I can" becomes "I knew I could."

This process repeats for each new project or campaign you create. It's the roller coaster ride of projects and it's both terrifying and fun!

Revisiting the Plan

Every plan needs a sanity check. Some questions to ask *before* you start the campaign:

- Is this the best plan to help us hit our numbers?
- Has our organization ever hit numbers like this?
- At what point do we check in and adjust if the numbers aren't where we want them?
- What happens when we do hit our numbers? How will we capitalize on that momentum? Pro tip: Ask for a raise!

During the campaign:

- Are we getting the uptake and participation from our partners that we wanted?
- What numbers should we be checking on a regular basis (visits, clicks, leads, etc.)?

After the campaign:

- In comparing our results against our initial assumption, how have we done? Have we achieved our goals?
- If not, why? How can we improve upon it later?

Feelings are good but facts are better. Setting SMART goals together helps organizations avoid the blame game when a program doesn't work and ensures that the credit for success is shared. Plus, everyone feels better when there's a plan. Know which partners you can count on. Allow yourself to adjust your expectations as you go and remember that measurement is the key to success.

ELEVEN

TROUBLESHOOTING YOUR CHANNEL

Despite your best efforts, things occasionally go wrong. Fortunately, many channel marketing problems are familiar and predictable. We'll address a few of the major ones in this chapter. If you're not experiencing any of these today, we're glad, but be ready! Chances are you will at some point and working to prevent them now will save you time, resources, and lots of unneeded stress.

Problem #1: Direct Sales Wants All Your Leads

Most companies with a reseller channel begin with a direct sales force and that team is well-established by the time the channel gets built. Direct sellers typically enjoy a lot of visibility (and glory) which can breed a sense of entitlement that can be tough to change.

The truth, however, is that if your partners are generating leads with their marketing efforts (or with your efforts on their behalf), then those leads belong to your partners, not the direct team. If your direct sales force circumvents your partners' efforts and acts on those leads, you shouldn't expect to keep your partners around very long.

You must advocate for your partners. It may take some coaching and education on your part with the management team, making everybody aware of the partners' value. Can direct sales do a better job closing any given lead? Probably. Selling your product is their primary responsibility and, for the typical partner, your product is probably one of many. But what gets lost in effectiveness gets made up for in scale. If you want to multiply your reach and drive more sales activity, you need to allow your partners to own their leads.

It helps if this trade-off doesn't result in a sacrifice for the direct sales team. Find a way to make working with your partners a win-win. For example, a compensation package that still rewards a direct seller for a sale made by a partner in his or her territory or account base will incentivize them to work *with* the channel. Let the sales team enjoy the fruits of scalability, too. Now, instead of working at cross-purposes, partners and direct sellers are working as teammates.

Problem #2: You're Trying to Control Your Partners

This is a hard one to recognize because your intentions are good and you're trying to be helpful. But there's a fine line between being helpful and being controlling. Here we return to relationship basics: It's easy to want to force your priorities onto your partners; you assume their priorities are the same as yours. You think you're on the same page until you notice that your partners aren't paying any attention to the plans you've made.

Partners have their own plans, their own priorities, and their own ideas of growth. Stop trying to own your partner's business and instead of forcing their alignment, find a way to align with them and their priorities.

Problem #3: Weak Executive Support

Lots of executives pay lip service to the importance of the channel but when push comes to shove, you find yourself and your partners ignored. You have the nagging feeling that the channel is just not that high of a priority. Worse, your fears are confirmed by a lack of funding.

This is often a maturity issue where, as we discussed above, the channel is relatively new compared to direct sales and the value just isn't well understood. In addition to the lack of support, the executive team may even approach the channel with the same kind of tight control they approach direct sales, not realizing the two need to be managed differently. But weak support can happen in any organization at any stage. It's another opportunity for coaching and education. Demonstrate your expertise and your grasp of your position. Show them your short-term and long-term plans and detail the activities that will, in time, give you results that are worthy of support.

Successful channel marketing leaders "manage up," framing their efforts in a way that help executives understand the importance of those efforts *to the company*. To a lot of executives, the inherent lack of control over the channel is a significant concern. The typical channel partner is out "there" somewhere, a wildcard working with a separate agenda. Your job is to let your executives know you have your finger on the pulse of the channel and that your company and its partners are moving forward in a mutually beneficial way.

In all your efforts to demonstrate value to the executive team, it helps to have an ally at their level. Take advantage of a relationship you may have with an executive who has a channel marketing background or who at least understands what you're trying to do. Someone on peer-level with other executives will provide you with a lot of credibility.

Problem #4: Not Enough Support from Other Parts of the Company

Even with executive support, you need help from other places too, like operations, IT, and product marketing. If they're not on board with your efforts, they can act as roadblocks.

There are two ways to get help. The first is the way most people ask—with no real agenda and no specific call to action, just vague ideas that get lost on the party being asked. We recommend the second way—a professional approach that is direct, strong, and specific. Put together a short briefing deck outlining your plans and strategy and the results you're trying to drive for the company. The key word is "short." It needn't be comprehensive but it does need to be detailed enough to make your audience understand the level of involvement necessary and what role they'll play. You'll present it to those from whom you'll need participation and to those from whom you'll need approval. By being professional and prepared, you'll be establishing expectations for each.

Create a short "walking" deck that provides an overview of your plans, metrics, and the level of involvement required from others. Use this to build support across the organization.[21]

For a valuable template for this, consider using a responsibility matrix like RACI—Responsible, Accountable, Consulted, and Informed[22]. Use it when you build your plans and in your deck so that everyone understands their part.

If nothing else, you'll demonstrate your careful planning and preparedness, and your audience will respond accordingly.

---

[21] You'll find a sample walking deck on our website at *marketingmultiplied-book.com*.
[22] Jacka, Mike; Keller, Paulette (2009). Business Process Mapping: Improving Customer Satisfaction. John Wiley and Sons.

People want to know where they fit in, why and, most importantly, to what end. A solid plan with clearly defined goals and responsibilities is always more effective than an ambiguous request for help.

If you still can't get the help you need (because the departments you need help from are either unwilling or unable), you'll at least be on the record as having tried. This will help you make the case to the executive level for further action or an increase in your budget so that you can get what you need yourself. Alternatively, you can consider using an outside agency to provide the pieces of the puzzle that you're not able to get internally.

Problem #5: Apathy, Inertia, or Lack of Action

This is easy enough to recognize in others around your organization but can you see it in yourself? Sometimes lack of action comes from a feeling of being overwhelmed, a consequence of having a weak or disorganized plan. Sometimes it comes from lack of motivation due to poor or nonexistent goal-setting. Whatever the source of your inertia, you must find a way to get unblocked. To take care of your channel, you first need to take care of yourself.

There are a lot of resources to help you find your motivation. A good first step is to check out the BestSelf Blog[23] for ideas. There's a lot there, but pick out the things you think will help you the most and the fastest. Find ways to get yourself moving forward.

---

[23] *blog.bestself.co*

When it comes to stasis in others within your company, it all gets back to framing your goals within the context of the company's needs. This dovetails with Problem #4 above: How is your plan going to help others in your organization, both the approvers and participants? How can you align with them for a common share of success? How can you make things easier for them? Nobody is looking for a second job, so if you want to motivate others around you, find ways to make it easy for them to engage.

Problem #6: You're Trying to be Everything to Everybody

It's natural to want to help your partners. You want to involve yourself and be there for them, conference with them, spend whatever time it takes to educate them and handhold them all the way to success. With five or ten or even twenty partners, this isn't outside the realm of possibility. With two hundred or two thousand partners? You're going to find yourself overwhelmed very quickly.

You need to make difficult choices about where to spend your time, knowing that you can't do it all. Play to your strengths, focusing your efforts where they're most effective for your partners, and finding other people to do the rest. Remember, you're not an agency, you're a channel marketer! You can find an agency to delegate to, or—often better—you can get your partners more involved in their own lead generation. We talked about it earlier in the book: if you do everything for your partners, they will come to expect it. You'll be teaching them dependence. But partners need to have skin in the game. Successful partnerships reflect parity. Be supportive and involved, but make sure your partners are involved as well. Your life will be a lot easier.

This is not an exhaustive list of the problems you are going to face but these are some of the most common. Recognizing a problem sooner rather than later will make for a faster rebound. Maybe you already see one or two of these in your company. The good news is that there are solutions and, by being prepared and paying attention, there's nothing you can't work around or power through.

HIRING AND MOTIVATING CHANNEL MARKETERS

Among all the tasks that channel leaders are responsible for, hiring is one of the most difficult. Sometimes it feels as if you're always hiring. As soon as your team is fully staffed, something changes and you're back in hiring mode. Just as difficult is retaining and motivating your staff, especially for Silicon Valley companies, where the next open seat in channel marketing is literally right around the corner. Let's consider the factors you should focus on to get the right people in the right positions, keep them there, and propel their success.

The Hiring Process

There is a multitude of factors to consider when making a hire but all of them revolve around these three: skills, experience, and values. How much of each you can find in any one candidate often depends on your budget, the specific needs of your business, and how long you're willing to wait.

Skills

If you have the financial resources, you can hire someone with channel marketing skills, and probably from your specific industry. A smaller budget may limit you to candidates who possess a softer set of skills, perhaps honed outside of your field, but that nevertheless provide the foundation for a good channel marketer.

Communication, for example, is a required skill. A successful channel marketer needs the ability to articulate verbally, of course, but also with the written word. Effective writing has become something of a lost art. In her book *Everybody Writes*, Ann Handley, Chief Content Officer of MarketingProfs states:

"Our writing can make us look smart or it can make us look stupid. It can make us seem fun, or warm, or competent, or trustworthy—or it can make us seem humdrum or discombobulated or flat-out boring. That's true whether you're writing a listicle or the words on a SlideShare deck..."[24] Accurately conveying ideas in writing requires organization skills and the ability to reason, qualifications that have valuable application elsewhere.

Communication can also mean video, graphic design, and social media skills. "Millennials" are recruited at a lot of companies for their social media skills alone. But knowing how social media works is not the same thing as knowing what to say. Find candidates who have a knack for knowing *what* to communicate, not just *how*.

Excellent negotiation skills are a must. Channel marketers manage partners, vendors, sales teams, and executives—and not everybody will always get what they want. These are relationships that must be navigated deftly.

Experience

Experience is closely aligned with skills and, again, will have a lot to do with your budget. Can you afford to hire someone who sharpened their skills in your industry in a channel marketing role? Or will the soft skills they learned elsewhere suffice?

Experience almost always comes more expensively but, depending on the maturity of your organization, it may be worth it. If your channel is relatively new, for instance, a seasoned leader who has successfully built a channel elsewhere can potentially save you years of struggles and mistakes. Instead of

---

[24] Handley, Ann, *Everybody Writes*, Wiley, 2014.

proceeding in fits and starts, you can leap ahead, right over the otherwise painful growth process.

But don't just hire someone because of their experience either. Remember that all candidates bring baggage through the door, and your job is to decide if it's a carry-on or a steamer trunk. As much good as a candidate may offer, they might also bring bad habits from previous companies. Think about the cultural fit within your organization. Are you a small, hyper-growth startup and the candidate is a seasoned channel marketer from an established firm? It's not hard to have success when you have huge budgets and resources but how will they react to having to work on a shoestring? Are they a "pointer" or a "doer" or both and what do you most need right now?

Someone with sales experience is valuable. Alignment between marketing and sales is critical and a candidate who understands the sales cycle and who has spent time close to the customer can be a tremendous asset. Understanding your customers' needs is a critical skill for a marketer and too few marketers have seen the transaction from the point of view of the buyer.

Values

All the skills and experience in the world won't help if your candidate doesn't possess the values needed to succeed as a channel marketer. The most important value? *Empathy.* Being sensitive to the needs and desires of others is a crucial characteristic of successful marketers and it's especially vital for a channel marketer. Empathy will guide your channel marketers from within. They'll do the right things for your partners and for your company. Without empathy, people only do things that are good for themselves, a sure recipe for long-term failure.

Look for candidates that are service-oriented and who find reward in serving others. Much of channel marketing is serving the needs of others, so find someone who understands this inherently. Skills can be taught, but the inclination to serve isn't nearly as teachable.

Determining value traits is often a matter of knowing how to frame your interview questions. Create a line of questioning that will help you identify whether your candidates have demonstrated empathy in the past, are oriented towards serving customer needs, and share the values your organization requires. You will find a good set of sample interview questions on our website.

Recognize that most candidates will say anything in an interview and can be notorious for discerning the intent of a question and responding to what the interviewer wants to hear. On a resume and in an interview, *everyone lies* or at least exaggerates a little. Explore the transition points in their resume; that's where the juicy stories are and the prospective employee's personality is revealed. Are they in the driver's seat of their career, or do they blame others for what happens to them? Would you bring them to a dinner party with your closest friends? Are you at ease with them? Have you controlled the interview, or have they?

We've also seen success with intelligence and personality tests, such as the Myers-Briggs Type Indicator, a personality inventory that helps determine which of sixteen personality types the candidate matches. There are many other tests available as well, and though they all have slightly different methodologies, they typically produce the same conclusions.

Recruiting

Before hiring comes the matter of where to find the candidates in the first place. The number one rule on recruiting and hiring is this: *never settle*. There are roughly 7.6 billion people on this planet and your perfect candidate is somewhere among them. It's tempting to want to fill the empty seat right away, especially when budgets can disappear without notice. Patience helps ensure that you don't make a mistake and repeat the painful (and expensive) hiring process.

Among the best sources of talent are the connections to your existing talent. A-players hang out with other A-players. If you have stars on your team, chances are they know other stars.

Responsibilities

What *specific* things will the people you hire be doing for you and your company? Draw clear lines of responsibility. You'll want to think very carefully about what each position entails before you fill it and that means mapping the various duties the job requires.

Most companies begin building their channel with a generalist, the new *Channel Marketing Manager* who starts things up, handles partner recruiting, campaign creation, partner enablement, and everything else. They develop the plan and execute it. This person might already work on the marketing or direct sales side of the company. Alternatively, it could be someone from the outside who has experience and the ability to think strategically to create a long-term vision. This is an excellent opportunity to be looking for that seasoned leader mentioned earlier, the person who has successfully created a channel and can steer the company past the potential hazards.

As a company's channel matures, there's often a need for more specialization. Specialization can be assigned by partner type, by product, by geography, or by whatever makes sense in your situation. You might, for example, have a specialist who does nothing but manage your distribution partners. Distributors have different needs than value-added resellers (VARs). Or maybe you have a specialist who manages your South-American partners, or even just your partners in Brazil, understanding the unique needs and culture of that locale.

Other channel organizations specialize by function. Partner communication, for example, is a specialization all its own. As companies grow, communication can become fractured, with partners getting mixed signals from various parts of your organization. It's important to have someone in place to ensure that the message to partners is consistent and that the company doesn't hammer them with a new offer every day.

Partner enablement is also a critical function. Who will be responsible for partner training, tools, and support services? The *Partner Enablement Specialist* knows the needs of the partners and works to ensure they're met.

A *Partner Experience Manager* is a position that has been recently gaining favor. This person's responsibility is to monitor the systems and processes that a company uses to interact with its partners. The goal of the Partner Experience Manager is to examine things from a partner's point of view and eliminate areas of friction. Interaction should be a harmonious and unified experience across your organization. Why does this matter? Because partners frequently complain about how difficult brands make it to do business with them and they gravitate towards brands that make their lives easier. Think of the different points of partner engagement with your company—from how they join your program, to how they communicate with you, how they do business planning with you, how deals are registered, how sales are processed, and everything in between. Engagement should be consistent and seamless. Here's a simple example you've probably seen yourself: The partner portal is one place; partner marketing is another. Configure, Price, and Quote (CPQ) is yet another system. Partners go to still another place to claim MDF. And each of these sites requires a different login and password! Now multiply this by the twenty-plus lines a partner carries. It seems like a trivial thing, but it is incredibly annoying to a partner. It's the job of the partner experience manager to eliminate unnecessary annoyances and to make sure the experience of dealing with your company is a smooth and efficient one.

Developing Talent

Getting the right people in the right roles is just the beginning. Your job now is to help them to grow and develop and to keep them challenged. This is done by coaching, and not just occasionally but continually. If someone on your team is surprised to learn bad news during their performance review, you're not managing them properly. There should be no surprises and no disconnect between you and your staff. Through weekly or biweekly one-on-ones, your team should always know where they stand. This doesn't mean micromanaging; you hired adults, after all. But it does mean recognizing the areas where you think it's appropriate to help them develop, to motivate them, and to unstick them if necessary.

One-on-ones shouldn't be cumbersome either. Returning to another lesson from Herold's *Double Double*, one-on-ones should be quick, and driven by a strong agenda, like so:

- Temperature Taking – how are they doing, professionally and personally? What's on their mind? Are they feeling overwhelmed and tired, or are they still excited about their job? This is a good icebreaker and gives you an opportunity to speak with them informally to get a sense for where they're at.

- Goals for Last Period – did they do what they said they would do? You're not asking so you can micromanage them; you're looking for ways to unstick them if they couldn't complete a goal. Remember, everyone works better with a plan!

- Goals for Next Period – what do they want to get done between now and your next meeting? No more than three items. These should be strategic, i.e., not things they would do anyway as part of their job. They should also be aligned with your organization's goals and/or company goals.

- Where are you stuck? If they're blocked, unblock them. You will get the most out of them when you focus on *energizing* and *unsticking* them.

- Skill Development – Saved for the end, it's an excellent opportunity to show them how to do something new or to set a goal for them to learn something on their own. Employees that are continuously learning stay in their jobs longer!

You should lead the discussion and keep notes, referring to them before future one-on-ones. We find this is particularly useful in the Temperature Taking section; it's an opportunity to circle back with them on a personal matter they might have shared a few weeks prior.

Good coaching can also involve giving a project to the less experienced person on the team, allowing them the chance to learn while doing and giving them the opportunity to push beyond their current limits. This requires monitoring and feedback to ensure the desired outcome. You can also have them "shadow" a more experienced teammate, either for a specific project or for a set period. Another useful development technique is to have your staff member experience a "day in the life" of a partner. Identify a local partner who would be willing to allow your staff member to follow them around for a day, to get a sense of how they work, how they sell, how they market themselves, and how they deliver. Seeing how your partners operate will be eye-opening, allowing for a greater understanding of the interests, motivations, and needs of the typical partner.

Ongoing training is vital. External sources of training will take you and your team out of your day-to-day world, and you will learn things that apply to your own processes. Cross-functional training is also valuable. When marketers take sales training, it helps build empathy, and it's also beneficial.

Getting the Most out of Your Team

As with channel partners, motivating channel marketers comes by way of appropriate incentives, preferably aligned with clear-cut key performance indicators (KPIs), aka goals. We see a lot of organizations pay bonuses based on achievement of annual KPIs but this means the team works hard for twelve months and hope they've hit their goals for that one-time bonus. Some people don't have the attention span. It's better to take annual KPIs and break them into quarters. Incentive compensation assigned to quarterly objectives means the team can see the fruits of their work as they go and it ties performance and compensation in a much more concrete way than an annual check.

Remember that incentives and rewards can take different forms than just monetary compensation. Employee recognition is always appreciated, and it can be tied to partner results, too. If an individual partner is doing well, everyone who touches that partner should be singled out and recognized.

There are many ways to tie incentives, monetary or otherwise, to performance. A channel marketer's scorecard can include how many partner plans were created, how many activities planned, how many executed, the results of each, and so forth. There are many other kinds of incentives, too. Besides monetary compensation and recognition, you can reward employees with prizes, trips, dinner with the CEO, or any number of awards, small and large, that will keep your channel team motivated, engaged, and happy.

THE CHANNEL MARKETING TOOLBOX

Like the best carpenters, successful channel marketers have the right tools. From partner communication to planning and tracking, you're going to want access to all the things that can help you succeed, not to mention make your life easier. Some resources are more expensive than others. Here we propose the must-have tools with options based on your budget.

Communication

A partner communication tool is the most essential in the tool-box. This goes beyond broadcasting to your partners. To create a vibrant partner ecosystem where you can support, enable, and engage with your partners, you need bi-directional communication, allowing your partners easy and efficient ways of connecting with you.

For many companies, it's an out of sight, out of mind problem. It's easy to take partners for granted, assuming they're out there, faithfully representing you, but don't be so sure. Let them know you're there for them and keep your company and your products top of mind for your partners. It doesn't need to be profound and awe-inspiring, it just needs to be there—something of value to keep your partners engaged and reminding them that you're ready to aid in their success.

Tools that allow for this include email, webcasts, conference calls, in-person events, office hours, and social media.

If it's in the budget: Partner Relationship Management (PRM) software is a cloud-based partner portal where you can effectively and efficiently manage your partner relationships and communications. Examples we like include Webinfinity, Mindmatrix, and Channeltivity. Not only do these work as partner portals, but they integrate with your CRM (Salesforce, for example), thereby allowing you to keep a line of sight on what your partners are doing.

If the budget is a bit more limited: Email is free. Other free or low-cost methods of communication include Skype, conferencing solutions like Zoom and GoToMeeting, and social media platforms like Twitter or LinkedIn where you can set up a private group as a forum for sharing information with partners and engaging in dialogue with them.

Lead Management and Deal Registration

The sharing of leads and the potential opportunities (deals) they lead to needs to be easy and efficient. You need a way to deliver your partners the leads you're generating from marketing campaigns and activities, and your partners need a way to ensure their deals are protected. You need a registration system that's dependable, user-friendly, and doesn't torture the partner with a fifty-field form.

If it's in the budget: Your PRM platform should have this capability. Integrated with your CRM application, efficient lead-sharing and registration will be assured and channel conflict will be minimized.

If the budget is a bit more limited: Leads can always be sent via email. Excel can be used to deliver a list of names from a tradeshow, for example. (Excel is our spreadsheet program of choice but Google Sheets is sufficient too.) Partners can register a lead via email, or, preferably, through a web capture form you've made available to them on your site. Alternatively, Google Forms or cloud-based applications like

SurveyMonkey can provide easy-to-use forms that your partners will appreciate.

The important part of this is the feedback. When a partner registers a deal, they want to know it's protected, both from other partners and your sales teams, and the feedback must be as close to real-time as it can be.

Training

In Chapter 4, we talked about skill building. Yes, training your partners in selling and marketing your products is critical. But no less important for your partners are the soft skills—sales, marketing, customer engagement, and basic business skills. To provide training, you need an effective delivery toolset and a wide variety of formats to appeal to the many ways in which your partners prefer to receive information. It's even more effective if your training comes with a way that allows you to measure what's getting through. Quizzes or incentive-based "levels" that partners need to attain can ensure that your material is hitting the mark.

If it's in the budget: Learning Management Systems (LMS) are available through software platforms like Litmos, SumTotal Systems, or Cornerstone OnDemand. With these systems, you can create training programs and testing. Reporting is a key feature of these programs and you can easily monitor the progress of your partners and align incentives and promotions accordingly. Learning modules can be customized for specific types of partners or for specific subjects. Is your company already using a software platform for internal training? See if you can expand or customize it to suit your partners' training needs. Some of the training may be very similar, after all.

If the budget is a bit more limited: Produce your own LMS. We find videos to be the most effective means of training and, fortunately, they're not hard—or expensive—to create. You can make your own videos and you don't need anything fancier than your webcam. You can record screen captures or create PowerPoint presentations and save them as MP4s. Post them on YouTube, set the privacy mode to "Unlisted", and send your partners the link to them. SurveyMonkey and Google Forms will work to test your partners' knowledge.

Marketing Planning

Good channel execution starts with a marketing plan, where you engage your partners in a thoughtful process to create definitive and measurable outcomes. This beats the "random acts of marketing" strategy we see most brands employing. Planning with your partners provides a focused approach that allows you to better align your resources.

It's also useful for sniffing out misunderstandings or potential points of disagreement. Maybe your partners have expectations of you that are unrealistic. Or vice-versa! Maybe your partners have unworkable (or just plain bad) ideas. Planning is an appropriate time to get everything on the table and find ways in which to match up your goals with your partners' goals. It's much better to accomplish this in planning mode than execution mode.

If it's in the budget: Platforms like Successful Channels are available to make your planning customized and comprehensive. CAM-led and integrated with your CRM platform, you'll have a robust planning framework that allows you to collaborate with your partners through screen share, and walks you both through a methodical process to create an effective marketing plan, complete with projected outcomes. An efficient reporting system allows you to continually measure performance against goals and make the right adjustments.

If the budget is a bit more limited: There's nothing wrong with using Word or Excel for planning. The key is to create a template that links tasks and activities to core goals and tactics. You'll want to be able to measure your success. Keep it simple and flexible.

MDF/BDF/Co-Op

As discussed in Chapter 9, money allocated to partners to help them drive demand can be very motivational. But whether it's a proposal-based or performance-based program, you'll need the means to execute and monitor it. You'll need a way to allow partners to make requests, show proof of performance, enable them to make claims, make payments to them, and track results.

If it's in the budget: E2Open's CIM software helps global brands with MDF, channel rebates, and sales incentives, and it can be configured to your business model and integrated with your CRM. The upshot is ease of use and comprehensive reporting.

If the budget is a bit more limited: Once again, Excel and Word can get the job done. Claims and requests can be made via Google Forms.

Incentives

Marketing and sales incentives designed to activate partners and get them further engaged can take a variety of forms as we discussed in Chapter 8. Whether the program is created to motivate your partners to launch a digital marketing campaign, take a training class, or drive registration for a customer conference, the key is to successfully and efficiently manage it.

If it's in the budget: Perks Worldwide offers a comprehensive and highly customizable platform for administering incentives, rebates, SPIFFs, and promotions. Corporate Rewards is another excellent vendor in this space, with a proven track record of success.

If the budget is a bit more limited: Electronic gift cards from the likes of Amazon and Starbucks cannot be overestimated. They're easy to buy and easy to deliver. We recommend you stay away from anything that requires a lot of hands-on work. As we mentioned in Chapter 8, sending t-shirts and hats sounds like a lot of fun until you find yourself stuck in a conference room all day stuffing boxes. And your programs can be managed on the cheap with Excel.

Digital Marketing

Enabling your partners to go to market with you means equipping them with the digital tools they need to generate demand. That's why you have partners in the first place. This could mean creating landing pages, sending out emails, generating social media content, creating website content, hosting events, engaging with agency partners, and anything else designed to help your partners attract leads and grow sales.

If it's in the budget: Leading the way in the channel marketing automation software space is Averetek. Sure, we're biased (this is our company), but Averetek provides a comprehensive set of solutions to make it easy for partners to engage in digital marketing.

If the budget is a bit more limited: Digital campaign materials can be delivered to your partners via Dropbox or Google Drive, allowing them to download everything they need to create their own digital marketing campaigns.

Your Planning and Partner Management Tools

The tools above are designed for your partners' engagement. But what about your own needs? What are the tools you need to organize your own workflow for planning and for partner management?

If it's in the budget: Look for planning and tracking programs like Trello, Asana, Microsoft Project, and ActiveCollab, each with its own set of advantages depending on your needs.

If the budget is a bit more limited: Craft your plan in PowerPoint for easy sharing and track your progress in Excel.

Tracking it All

You need a way to keep track of *everything*. Your success depends on measuring performance, collecting the relevant data points and having a reporting scorecard that you can use to gauge progress. Your toolbox needs to include tracking mechanisms so that you can see where your organization is today and where it's headed.

Think about the rhythm of your business. How often do you want to update your metrics? Quarterly? Monthly? Weekly? An automated system is ideal. If you're updating your metrics manually, make sure to build the time into your calendar. You'll need it to extract the information as well as run the desired analyses. And if you're relying on numbers from other people, make sure to allow for the time necessary to collect the data you need.

If it's in the budget: Domo is an excellent platform for collecting and analyzing data. So are Tableau and Grow.com. All are user-friendly and interactive and offer customized reporting complete with great visualizations.

If the budget is a bit more limited: Excel once again comes to the rescue. It's more work but it can be made easier if you commit to it, block out time for it, and make sure everybody's on board with the idea of delivering to you the data that you need in a timely way.

Considerations

Implementing the tools above must be done wisely and with care. There are a few considerations you'll need to think through.

Eliminate friction wherever possible. Make sure the tools you use integrate with each other. You want everything to be seamless for your partners. Don't give them a myriad of different URLs to visit for different tools, each with its own separate login and password. Find a way to bring all your partner engagement tools under one roof and make it easy for your partners to engage with you.

Integrate data sources. Another way to reduce friction. Make reporting easy for your partners and don't make them fill out forms with questions you already know the answers to.

Streamline where possible, and if partner information changes, make sure it changes across your partner program.

Be transparent. Allow your partners to access as much information as is reasonable. Where can they find a product manual? What is the status of a given lead? What are their sales numbers for the quarter? When will their rebate arrive? Help them help themselves. The more they can quickly find on their own, the less time will be spent in back and forth communication. (And the more willing they'll be to engage.)

Make engagement easy. Are your partners able to interact with you easily and in *their* preferred manner? Make sure direct communication is simple and responsive whether it's email, phone, or chat, and make it available every way you can. Finally, make sure your toolset is accessible across a variety of devices (desktop, tablet, mobile, etc.).

Where do I start?

We know there are a lot of ideas here and it can be a little overwhelming to think about deploying all of these tools. So, what's your starting point? How do you get underway?

Start with inventory. What are the capabilities you now have and what don't you have? You don't have to acquire the whole toolbox at once. Prioritize. Consider the above a checklist for tools you ultimately want to deploy, then decide what's most important and start there.

Do you have these tools already? Then measure them against the level of engagement you want from your partners. Are your tools working, in other words? Are they optimized? Are they being utilized to their maximum potential? Ask yourself if you're getting everything you can out of your partner toolbox. Tools need to be sharpened every now and then. Make sure you're getting the most out of yours.

For any budget, the right tools exist. This isn't an exhaustive list but if you can find a way to add the tools in this chapter to your toolbox, you'll make life a whole lot easier for you and your channel.

CONTINUING DEVELOPMENT

If you're investing the time to read this book, we probably don't have to emphasize the importance of ongoing education. You understand that success in the long term requires a steady stream of fresh ideas and you've likely seen how disastrous for a career complacency can be. Groupthink often plagues organizations, making it vital to get outside of the typical venues of influence.

The better educated you are, the more equipped you'll be to promote and validate your ideas within your company. You'll gain credibility with those whose support you'll need to advance your agenda.

So, what are some excellent sources of ongoing education? It may be obvious but start with your own company and take advantage of the *internal programs* that are already in place. If you work for a mid-sized to large company, there may be educational resources and programs available to you. The training may be geared to direct sales/marketing and not channel marketing but don't let that deter you. Your channel partners are direct marketers, after all, and it pays to learn about the latest trends and methodologies in how they market and sell. You'll be better equipped to know how to work with them.

Industry Reports

Industry reports often provide a useful source of the macrotrends affecting your marketing effectiveness. Here is a handful that we find useful:

- Averetek's *State of Channel Marketing* includes many relevant details on channel marketing, including content effectiveness across partner regions and tiers.

- HubSpot makes available a *State of Inbound Marketing* report.
- Marketo's *State of Engagement* report is a helpful publication.
- IBM's Silverpop publishes excellent email marketing benchmarks.

Free Training

There are many training programs available for little or no charge. Hubspot offers an *Inbound Marketing Certification* complete with several hours of video training and quizzes, and the course includes strategies to align with the buyer's journey, from creating content and optimizing your website to ensuring customer delight. Best of all, it's free. They also have an *Inbound Sales Certification* and, although you may be a marketer, keeping yourself up to speed on sales will help you relate to the day-to-day business of your channel partners.

There's another benefit to education and training that focuses on direct marketing and selling: because direct marketers are on the ground, they often see industry trends first. Channel marketing overall frequently lags. Keeping up with the latest in direct marketing allows you to reduce your reaction time with the programs you offer your partners.

Analyst Groups and Conferences

Your company may subscribe to research from analyst groups as a source of frameworks, methodologies, and industry trends.

SiriusDecisions, The Channel Company, Baptie & Company, and Forrester Research are organizations that provide research-based analysis and insights. Along with other sources like industry reports, you can develop an understanding of trends that might affect your strategies.

These analyst groups host conferences too. You can glean valuable ideas from the keynotes and breakout sessions to inspire your plans. We find that events like Baptie & Co.'s Channel Focus series, which are specifically focused on the channel, strike an appropriate balance between content presented by channel professionals and vendors and you can learn a lot from both.

An additional benefit of attending a conference is the networking opportunity with vendors and your peers. Channel marketing is a small world and it's good to have friends!

Peer Training and Shadowing

In fact, you might consider taking peer relationships you've forged at a conference up a notch and this is where *peer training* can be very productive. Assemble a mastermind group and hold regular networking sessions with people who experience the same sort of challenges as you.[25] A mastermind group facilitates knowledge-sharing, brainstorming, support, and accountability. If you don't know where to get started with this, you might consider asking your favorite vendor to assist you. You're probably not their only client, and they should be able to facilitate

---

[25] For tips on getting this started, check out this link: *http://www.chrisducker.com/how-to-organize-a-mastermind-session/*. Additional links on Mastermind groups can be found on our website in the Resources section.

a session of people with similar job titles who can help and mentor you, while you do the same for them. You might ask the vendor to put together the first one and you can take the reins from there. These don't need to be in-person events; video conferences work just as well.

Peer training can also take the form of job shadowing. We wrote in Chapter 12 about shadowing experienced members of your company, or even a partner, for a day. Find people within or outside of your organization to spend time with. Many channel marketers work with a variety of role players in their jobs and we find the most successful channel marketers are those who have experience in those roles themselves. Get to know the people you interact with—what they do, how they do it, their problems, and how they overcome them. Sitting down with your marketing VP, for example, to better understand how your company generates leads and routes them to sales will help you understand the challenges your partners face with this process and you'll be in a better position to help them with the programs you launch and the results you generate. The more you know of all the facets involved in your product's development, marketing, sales, and fulfillment, the better you'll be as a channel marketer.

Become a student of the game—for your company, and for your career. Those that teach earn the right to sell and, as we've discussed throughout this book, there are many times when you will need to sell, whether it's to your channel partners, your managers, or your senior leaders. To do so successfully, you need to create teaching moments for your audience and, to do that, you must learn yourself, and *keep* learning.

CONCLUSION

At the beginning of this book, we mentioned three goals we wanted to accomplish. The first was to provide you with a framework to efficiently organize your marketing efforts. Underpinning this framework is the importance of aligning your marketing efforts with the modern buyer's journey. Marketing communication today needs to be positioned within the context of *learning, buying, shopping,* and *recommending,* and smart brands tell their story *to, with, through,* and *for* their channel partners. These are the fundamental dynamics of successful channel marketing in today's world. If you're in sync with the modern buyer's journey, and you're communicating your product's value in the right way given your partner relationships, you're on the right path.

The second goal was to give you practical tools and resources that you can apply to your business today and refer to when you get stuck. We hope you found some ideas for how to get partners to engage, how to measure your programs, how to build a team, and how to get stuff done, no matter your budget.

The final goal was to extend this book into an online community to help you with ideas and inspiration as the market changes and as you grow in your career. Channel marketing is a small world and you're not alone. There are many talented professionals and, in our experience, they're often willing to help others. Our vision is to build a community of peers and you can learn more about this initiative and get involved yourself at *marketingmultiplied-book.com*. We look forward to seeing you there.

People ask us all the time where they should begin. Our advice is to first document the vision of what you want your channel to look like two years from now. What is the revenue contribution from your partners? What geographies do you serve? What do your partners say about your program? What does your workday look like? By asking and answering questions like this, you are documenting your vision of the future. From there you can build a project plan that incorporates the framework and advice offered here and makes your vision a reality.

And if you start to doubt, or just need a little advice along the way, please track us down. We'd love to hear from you.

GRATITUDE

Thank you, Amy. You are my very best friend, confidant, and guiding light. All things are possible with you by my side. I love you.

Thanks NJ, Nate, Carmen, and Aubrey. You listen to my work stories and pretend to be interested. You have learned well from your mother!

To my Dads—Michael, my steady business partner through it all, and Steve, who is always cheering me on—thank you.

To Mike, my constant collaborator and first client, you opened my eyes to the problems software can solve for channel marketers and helped me create a career. Thank you.

I'm grateful for our clients, including Meaghan Sullivan, Lisa Penn, Liz Martin, Luanne Tierney, Helda Lopes, Anne Colbeck, Kael Kelly, Liz Anderson, Sheralyn Felix, Kristina Scott, Sean Donnelly, Jessica Walker McFarland, Kristi Houssiere, Steve Pataky, Michele Campbell, and many others that gave us an opportunity to serve and learn from them.

Thanks Guy Arama and Brian Gilbert for reviewing early drafts and providing us with excellent fact-checking and feedback.

Cameron Herold, your coaching changed the way I looked at the role of the CEO. Thank you.

Finally, I'm so grateful for the entire Averetek team: I am lucky to work beside this group of consummate professionals.

—Peter

To Denise. You've made all my dreams come true, even ones I didn't know I had.

To my children Alyssa, Megan, and Danny. You may not understand what channel marketing is but you're the reason I do it.

To my mother and sister. Thank you for your love and support.

To Peter, I'm always impressed by your willingness to take chances. Why not write a book together? Well, here we are.

To John Hollinger, an important mentor in my career. You taught me what it means to be a channel partner and so much more. I use your advice daily.

To Rob Gual, Dean Leonard, Marie Hutchins, Tom Monahan, Bob Lincavicks, Debby Keniry, and Kathy Cronin for welcoming me to the team that brought Microsoft on the road around New England. I learned so much about how to work with channel partners from you and had a lot of fun doing it.

To the Averetek team, which does so much to help our clients, I'm honored to work with such a dedicated team.

To my collaborators along the way—Todd Stallard, John Schuerenberg, Chris Large, Greg Lissy, Neal Wadhwani, Lesley Rubin, Steve Measelle, Dina Apostolou, Laura Stanton, Michael Grady, Liz Siver, Brad Rozen, Jay Roxe, Mike Porter, Rick Lacroix, Jennifer Ortiz, Paul O'Sullivan, and Jennifer Smith—you're a brilliant bunch and I've learned so much from working with you all.

–Mike

INDEX

ABOUT THE AUTHORS

Marketing Multiplied is a collaboration between Mike Moore and Peter Thomas. Mike and Peter's combined experience of more than forty years in the channel, and the work they've done with and for brands has shaped the perspective that is expressed in this book. Mike and Peter met in 2004 while Mike worked for Microsoft and Peter ran a software development firm. Peter and his team developed a through-partner event management platform to support Mike's vision. It was one of the first channel marketing software applications in the industry. Through their work on that project, Mike and Peter developed an extraordinary partnership of learning and creativity that eventually led to Mike joining Peter's company, Averetek, in 2014.

Mike Moore

Mike serves as Averetek's VP of Channel Strategy. Mike has spent twenty-three years in the IT channel as a channel partner and as a channel and field marketer for software companies like Microsoft, GE Healthcare, and Progress Software.

Mike lives in the Boston area with his wife Denise and their three children.

Connect with Mike on LinkedIn or Twitter.

Peter Thomas

Peter Thomas is the founder and CEO of Averetek, a channel marketing agency. Peter has spent more than twenty years helping channel leaders realize the potential of their partners using the magic of software.

Peter lives in the Boston area with his wife Amy and their four children.

Connect with Peter on LinkedIn or Twitter.

Made in the USA
Monee, IL
21 July 2021